WORSHIP
IN THE
SPIRIT OF
JESUS

D1611659

WORSHIP
IN THE
SPIRIT OF
JESUS

THEOLOGY, LITURGY, AND SONGS
WITHOUT VIOLENCE

JACK NELSON-PALLMEYER
AND BRET HESLA

THE
PILGRIM
PRESS
Cleveland

ACKNOWLEDGMENTS

The authors would like to thank the following people for their help during the writing of this book: Dave Gagne, Eleanor and John Yackel, Jaimie Bennett, Patricia Lundeen, and Sara Nelson-Pallmeyer.

The Pilgrim Press, 700 Prospect Avenue
Cleveland, Ohio 44115-1100, U.S.A.
thepilgrimpress.com

© 2005 by Jack Nelson-Pallmeyer and Bret Hesla

Illustrations by Bret Hesla

All rights reserved. Published 2005

Printed in the United States of America on acid-free paper

10 09 08 07 06 05   5 4 3 2 1

Library of Congress Cataloging-in-Publication Data

Nelson-Pallmeyer, Jack.
    Worship in the spirit of Jesus : theology, liturgy, and songs without violence /
Jack Nelson-Pallmeyer and Bret Hesla.
       p. cm.
    Includes bibliographical references.
    ISBN 0-8298-1674-7 (pbk.)
    1. Worship programs. 2. Nonviolence – Religious aspects – Christianity. 3. Jesus
Christ – Person and offices. I. Hesla, Bret, 1957- II. Title.
BV15.N45 2005
264 – dc22

2005040572

CONTENTS

Part Three
RESOURCES FOR
TALKING, PRAYING, WORSHIPING

PART ONE

JESUS' CHALLENGE
TO VIOLENCE

INTRODUCTION TO
PART ONE

MY FAITH JOURNEY

I (Jack) remember being disturbed by some of the Bible stories and religious songs I learned as a child. Drawing pictures of and singing about cute animals and a quaint ark could not fully divert my attention from troubling images of a violent God who declared creation "very good" and then deliberately destroyed the world and most of humanity. I was also told that babies who died before being baptized burned in hell. This seemed both sad and unfair. Singing "Jesus Loves Me" was comforting, but I received so many fear-inducing messages about the character of God from Bible passages, Sunday school teachers, pastors, and hymns that I was left confused and more than a little afraid. My classmates and I dutifully memorized Bible verses during confirmation classes while sitting in silence under the watchful eye of a stern pastor. I once mustered the courage to ask why a loving God would need to have Jesus killed in order to save us. This and similar questions weren't welcome.

I loved the community experience of my high school church youth group, but at college I realized we had never engaged pressing issues. Even national and international issues of profound magnitude, such as the civil rights movement and the war in Vietnam, had passed us by. My first real encounter with these issues and with the radical Jesus of the Gospels was during college. I returned to my church one Sunday to preach a sermon in which I said that Jesus' call to love enemies and be peacemakers couldn't be reconciled with saturation bombing, napalm, cluster bombs, and elevated body counts. Support for the war ran high, and one angry parishioner, reflecting the views of many, told me that if I objected to war then I shouldn't be a Christian. He challenged me to read the Bible, which he said was filled with stories about a violent God who used war to carry out God's purposes. I later discovered that he was right about frequent portrayals of God's purposeful violence, but I wasn't ready to abandon Christianity, which was and continues to be my spiritual home. The radical nonviolence of Jesus I glimpsed at the time was inspiring. I was embarking on a long journey seeking to understand why Jesus' life and teachings clashed so sharply with the values and attitudes of many Christians and with other violent images and expectations of God found in the Bible.[1]

Years later, during seminary, my awareness of Jesus deepened as did my suspicion that his experiences of God conflicted with biblical portrayals of God's redemptive or punishing violence. Time spent in India, Ethiopia, and urban Chicago as an undergraduate student at St. Olaf College led me to focus my seminary studies on the politics and religious dimensions of hunger.[2] This in turn drew me into the social justice demands of the biblical prophets. The prophets declared the causes of hunger, poverty, and oppression to be unjust systems dominated by the rich and powerful. They also challenged religious complicity with injustice and called people to change their lives and social systems in order to better reflect God's desired justice.

I found the social critique of the prophets insightful, and part of me lived vicariously through their anger that reflected my own frustration with many Christians who seemed indifferent or hostile to the political dimensions of hunger. Putting the common denominator of our anger and social critique aside, however, I was troubled by the terrifying images of God that were foundational to prophetic concerns, demands, and hopes. The prophets declared, for example, that God orchestrated historical catastrophes, including Israel's destruction, as punishment for social sins (see chapter 1). I probed in one paper what it would mean for God to punish us in a manner similar to the way the prophets portrayed God's judgment on the people of Israel. We lived in a nuclear age, in a hungry world, and in a nation whose policies and unjust systems seemed remarkably similar to those that had enraged the prophets. The answer was simple: catastrophe.[3]

Social justice concerns are clearly central to the Hebrew scriptures and to Jesus and should be a vital part of authentic Christian life. It seemed to me, however, that aspects of the Jesus story embedded in the Gospels suggested that although Jesus shared justice concerns with the prophets, he rejected their assertions that human or divine violence were the means to justice. Jesus embraced nonviolence and taught love of ene-mies. I was struggling with the realization that Jesus seemed to understand God's power differently than the prophets, many other biblical writers, and most of us.

Most religious traditions invite us into a deeper awareness and relation-ship to the presence of God. We must ask ourselves, however, whether the divine presence is violent or nonviolent, coercive or invitational, and whether living within the divine presence leads us to seek justice and peace through violent or nonviolent means. Jesus experiences the pres-ence of God as an invitation to justice *and* as the fountain of his radical nonviolence.

This insight concerning competing notions of power was undoubtedly connected to an experience I had as an undergraduate student in Calcutta, India. I walked through streets that often seemed like an earthly hell silently screaming at God, "How can you tolerate such suffering?" God seemed to not so silently answer back that the real question was why and how I and so many others could tolerate such suffering and still claim to be people of faith. At seminary in the context of my paper on the prophets, I felt that if God's character and power were violent and punishing as the prophets said, then we were doomed. Hope for the world seemed to depend on the prophets being wrong about God's punishing violence. In Calcutta, I began sensing that God's power was more invitational than coercive. God's power seemed to be restricted or enhanced by the work of my own hands.

My concerns about violent images of God and their distorting conse-quences for faith deepened after I graduated from seminary. My wife was reading the Bible cover to cover (something I had never done) over the course of a year one day at a time. Almost daily she shared passages in which divine or human violence was featured centrally, passages I had somehow managed to screen out or justify during years of biblical studies. Even as she shared multiple examples of dysfunctional biblical violence and despite my own history of being troubled by violent images of God, I

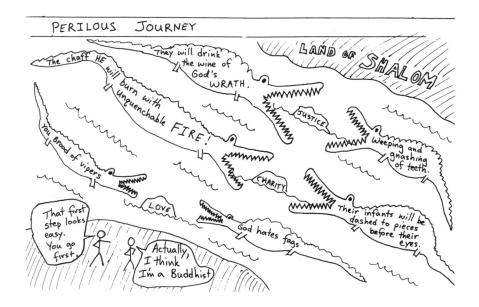

was still reluctant to explore the full implications of their meaning. When I finally embarked upon a cover-to-cover reading of the Bible I found it sobering, depressing, necessary, and fruitful. The full weight of the violence at the heart of both the Old Testament and the New was overwhelming, but it also brought into sharper focus a contrasting nonviolent stream of thought linked to the historical Jesus, a stream largely ignored by the Gospel writers and most of Christianity.

Reading the Bible cover to cover proved a decisive step in my religious journey. I came to see that the Bible contains diverse and incompatible portraits of God and Jesus and that as people of faith we have no good choice but to choose between irreconcilable portraits. Put simply, I realized that the biblical writers (and therefore the Bible itself) are often wrong about God and that we must sift through competing images of God and Jesus in light of our own religious experiences. The biblical writers are no different than us in that we, like them, try to make sense out of our lives and history in relationship to the divine presence. These thoughts, scary for me at the time and still unthinkable for many Christians, are now the central themes in my theology.[4] They also, as will be seen in the pages that follow, have profound implications for the content of our theology, worship, music, and liturgies.

Violence in the Bible and the Christian tradition were and are not my only concerns. As noted above, I have long been troubled by destructive U.S. foreign policies that have generally been supported by Christians. Many Christians consciously or unconsciously embrace a popular idea that has deadly consequences, namely, that superior violence saves. More than fifty thousand U.S. soldiers and millions of Vietnamese, Cambodians, and Laotians died in Indochina. For part of the 1980s, I lived in Central America, where hundreds of thousands of people, mostly civilians, were killed, disappeared, or tortured in the context of U.S.-sponsored "low-intensity wars."[5] Although the Vietnam War eventually proved unpopular and divisive, presidents and politicians count on war to give them a boost in the polls. They are rarely disappointed. George W. Bush's popularity soared during the wars with Afghanistan and Iraq (although this may change over time), as had his father's during the first Gulf War and the U.S. invasion of Panama.

It is disturbingly ironic that while Jesus rejected violence, taught love of enemies, and called his followers to be peacemakers, and although 84 percent of U.S. adults identify themselves as Christian, the United States now spends more money on the military than the rest of the world combined! There are many factors that explain the contradiction between the nonviolence of Jesus and Christian support for violence, but I believe a theological problem lies at its heart. Traditional Christian theology, worship, music, and liturgies generally downplay the nonviolent God of a nonviolent Jesus while reinforcing violent images of God. This pattern encourages us to ignore our vocation as peacemakers, makes us susceptible to the view that power is to be equated with violent power, and seduces us into complicity with destructive foreign policies.

VIOLENT IMAGES OF GOD

Many Christians today are troubled by violence in our world, and a significant minority opposes U.S. militarization. There is also growing

> Traditional Christian theology, worship, music, and liturgies generally downplay the nonviolent God of a nonviolent Jesus while reinforcing violent images of God. This pattern encourages us to ignore our vocation as peacemakers, makes us susceptible to the view that power is to be equated with violent power, and seduces us into complicity with destructive foreign policies.

awareness of a relationship between religion and violence, although Christians tend to see this as a problem for others. Many Jews, Christians, and Muslims are reluctant to acknowledge that the problem of religiously legitimated violence is related to violence in their "sacred" texts.[6] In the case of Christianity, violent images and expectations of God permeate our theology, worship, music, and liturgies. Assessing how and why this happened, describing consequences, and promoting alternatives rooted in the nonviolent spirit of Jesus are central themes in this book.

Christians have three compelling reasons to challenge and find alternatives to the violent images of God that dominate the Bible and much of our tradition. First, there are many Christians, including the present authors, who are dissatisfied with traditional Christian theology, worship, music, and liturgies that often reflect and reinforce violent images of God. These images feel alien to our own (Jack's and Bret's) religious experiences. Second, Jesus' life and teachings challenge these violent images. The radical nonviolence of Jesus (see chapter 3) offers a firm foundation for a re-ritualized Christianity (Part Two). Finally, violent images of God and violent traditions spill over into our world that is fracturing under the weight of violence, much of it justified in God's name.

Chapter 1 looks at the issue of religion and violence and demonstrates that violent images of God are at the heart of the three most important biblical story lines — Exodus, Exile, and the Apocalyptic worldview. Chapter 2 looks at Jesus' social world in order to provide a context for the radical challenges Jesus poses to these traditions. Chapter 3 explores a nonviolent stream penned by the New Testament writers in which Jesus

breaks with violent expectations of God and history. Chapter 4 documents how the theology of the New Testament writers largely ignores this non-violent stream as they, and much of traditional Christianity, interpret the meaning of Jesus' life and death through violent images of God that Jesus himself rejected. It also makes the case for why we need to re-ritualize Christianity, which sets the stage for Parts Two and Three, in which we offer alternative worship settings, liturgies, readings, and music that reflect the nonviolent spirit of Jesus. This introduction and each of chapters 1–4 include discussion questions and a suggested group activity. Ideas and guidelines for discussion leaders are found in Resource A below on pages 146–148.

DISCUSSION

Our Focus: To reflect on our faith journeys and to build momentum for discussing core topics.

Discuss one or more of the questions in each of the four categories.

Objective Questions

1. The author speaks of his own faith journey and his growing discomfort with violence in scripture and worship. Which of his struggles or experiences were most striking to you?

2. What were some important faith milestones or questions for the author in his life?

Reflective Questions

3. What feeling stood out for you as you read the introduction? Where did you find yourself feeling uncomfortable? Where did you find yourself feeling similar to the author?

4. What biblical stories do you most remember from childhood? What images of God were used in these stories? How did you make sense of violent descriptions of God when you were a child?

Interpretive Questions

5. The author describes his journey of faith. Think of where you are in your "faith journey." What questions do you have now about the nature of God? Which of the issues or struggles raised by the author seem most important to you? To this congregation? To youth?

6. Are there descriptions of God and God's action in the Bible you don't especially want young children to hear? If so, what are those descriptions and stories and what are the implications of your discomfort?

7. What, if any, are good reasons for Christians to reassess our tradition?

8. Can you think of any places where violent images of God appear in the church's theology and your congregation's theology and worship? Name those places. What do you think about these violent images of God?

Decisional Questions

9. How would a discussion of violence in religion affect our congregation? Can we talk about this topic in a healthy way? Where should we go with this topic?

ACTIVITY

Draw your faith journey. Using blank paper and a pencil draw a simple "faith timeline" of your life. For each decade, try to remember a particularly important and difficult faith struggle for you. When finished, gather in groups of three or four people and compare and discuss your timelines.

NOTES

1. Thirty years later I wrote a book about this mystery. See Jack Nelson-Pallmeyer, *Jesus against Christianity: Reclaiming the Missing Jesus* (Harrisburg, Pa.: Trinity Press International, 2001).

2. I focused much of my theological work during seminary on the issue of hunger, which culminated in my first book. See Jack Nelson, *Hunger for Justice: The Politics of Food and Faith* (Maryknoll, N.Y.: Orbis Books, 1980).

3. Explanations abound that historical catastrophes reflect the will and actions of a punishing God. Recent examples include Jerry Falwell and Pat Robertson saying that the terrorist attacks of September 11, 2001, were a sign that "God almighty is lifting his protection from us" because of feminists, abortionists, and the American Civil Liberties Union, as well as preachers in Central America explaining Hurricane Mitch as God's punishment for sin.

4. See *Jesus against Christianity*.

5. Jack Nelson-Pallmeyer, *War against the Poor: Low Intensity Conflict and Christian Faith* (Maryknoll, N.Y.: Orbis Books, 1989).

6. Jack Nelson-Pallmeyer, *Is Religion Killing Us? Violence in the Bible and the Quran* (Harrisburg, Pa.: Trinity Press International, 2003), xiv

CHAPTER 1

VIOLENT SCRIPTURES, VIOLENT WORLD

This is a painful chapter for me (Jack) to write, and it will be disturbing for many readers. It raises many unpleasant issues concerning religion and violence, including discussion of the violent images of God that dominate the Bible and much of the Christian tradition. Many of us may have thought about some of these issues and felt uncomfortable with violent images of God. Unfortunately, we have rarely been encouraged to verbalize our concerns or probe their implications and consequences for faith, worship, or our approach to the Bible. Although painful and disturbing, this chapter is necessary. We can appreciate fully the significance of the radical nonviolence of Jesus (chapter 3) and its implications for a re-ritualized Christianity (chapter 4, Parts Two and Three) only if we confront honestly the many violent images of God in the Bible.

RELIGION AND VIOLENCE

The beautiful world we celebrate as a gift from God is engulfed in nasty conflicts with religious roots. Religious dimensions of violence are evident in the divide separating Protestants and Catholics in Northern Ireland, the repression of base Christian communities in Latin America by military governments backed by Christian fundamentalists and the U.S. government,[1] the breakup and ethnic cleansing in former Yugoslavia, the deadly conflict between Christians and Muslims in the Sudan, Jewish occupation of Palestine justified with biblical references to the "chosen people," Muslim suicide bombers resisting Israeli occupation, and Hindus and Muslims killing each other over disputed land (Kashmir) and disputed sacred sites in India.

The task of understanding how and why religion encourages violence is complicated by two factors. First, people rarely kill each other over religious differences alone. They use God and religion to justify violence and killing, however, when conflicts escalate over land, oppression, discrimination, or other historical grievances. Second, people rarely challenge pervasive violence within their "sacred" texts. They may condemn religious violence, but many are unwilling to acknowledge that people can *reasonably* use religion to justify violence because the Bible, the Quran, and other "sacred" texts contain many violence-legitimating passages and many violent images of God.[2]

CHRISTIAN DENIAL

Christians generally avoid dealing with pervasive biblical violence and how it seeps into our tradition. One strategy employed is to ignore the violence or unconsciously reinforce it. The assumption seems to be that if something is in the Bible it must *somehow* be true and so we end scriptural readings with words such as "thanks be to God" or "this is the word of the Lord," no matter how brutal the story or violent the image of God may be. Another avoidance technique is to assert, against the evidence, that God is violent in the Old Testament but loving in the New Testament. Sanitizing violence also minimizes it. Draw pictures of animals and arks and turn away from drowning humanity. Interpret Jesus' death as a sacrifice arranged by a loving God and ignore troubling questions about why a loving God needs an atoning sacrifice. Treat the Exodus as a story of liberation and turn a blind eye to divinely sanctioned genocide.

Skipping over troubling verses is another avoidance strategy. I call this common practice lectionary gymnastics. In my church on a recent Sunday, for example, we read from Deuteronomy 11 but left out verses 23–25:

> ... then the Lord will drive out all these nations before you, and you will dispossess nations larger and mightier than yourselves. Every place on which you set foot shall be yours. ... No one will be able to stand against you; the Lord your God will put the fear and dread of you on all the land on which you set foot, as he promised you.

We can add to these approaches the fallback positions of citing mystery and metaphor. In the case of mystery we rightly assert that humans can't fully understand God and wrongly conclude that in the absence of full knowledge we shouldn't challenge God's violence. In relying upon metaphor we presume that the violence in the text refers to something other than real violence. I once attended a national conference of nonviolent Catholic peace activists who enthusiastically sang songs about God drowning Pharaoh's army in the Red Sea! Collectively these strategies legitimize or diminish the impact of violence to the point that an honest assessment of how violent images of God have deeply impacted our theology, worship, music, liturgies, and *understanding of power* becomes impossible, as does assessing their relationship to a violent world.

SELECTIVE CONCERNS

The terrorist attacks of September 11, 2001, and the wars that followed brought issues related to religion and violence to the forefront. Osama bin Laden's terror-justifying rhetoric was "saturated with religious argument and theological language."[3] So too were the speeches of President George W. Bush and his advisors, who justified retaliatory actions with words eerily similar to those of bin Laden. Each side defined the conflict as a struggle between good and evil. Each justified civilian casualties because the depraved other could be countered only with lethal violence. Each invoked God's name to ground the righteousness of their cause.[4] Each believed their violent actions were faithful responses to their "sacred" texts or traditions.

Andrew Sullivan wrote that people were initially reluctant to discuss religious dimensions of the conflict following the terror attacks:

> It seems almost as if there is something inherent in religious mono-
> theism that lends itself to this kind of terrorist temptation. And our
> bland attempts to ignore this — to speak of this violence as if it did
> not have religious roots — is some kind of denial. We don't want
> to denigrate religion as such, and so we deny that religion is at the
> heart of this. But we would understand this conflict better, perhaps,

if we first acknowledged that religion is responsible in some way, and then figure out how and why.[5]

Reticence to discuss religion and violence seems to have passed. In a December 2003 Minnesota Poll, "77 percent of respondents attributed at least a fair amount of the cause of the world's wars and conflict to religion."[6] The issue at present, particularly for Christians, is our tendency to see religion and violence as a problem for others and not ourselves. Respondents to the Minnesota Poll, for example, focused the discussion of religion and violence almost exclusively on Islam. When "asked about specific religions, 34 percent said that Islam is more likely to encourage its believers to be violent, compared with 3 percent for Christianity, 5 percent for Judaism, 5 percent for Buddhism and 7 percent for Hinduism."[7]

I think it is appropriate to raise serious questions about Islam and violence. There are numerous violent themes in the Quran and some Muslims specifically cite the Quran to justify their violent actions.[8] Problems arise because many Christians concerned about Islam and violence are unaware that their "Christian nation" is the most militarized country in the history of the world.[9] It is easy to turn a blind eye to our nation's violence and to deny that there may be a relationship between Christian support for militarization and war and traditional Christian theology, worship, music, and liturgies that downplay Jesus' radical nonviolence while embracing violent images and expectations of God. A narrow focus on Islam, in other words, ignores what may arguably be the greater problem of Christianity and violence. As Jesus once said, "You hypocrite, first take the log out of your own eye, and then you will see clearly to take the speck out of your neighbor's eye" (Luke 6:42).[10]

Poll results that limit concern about religion and violence to Islam run counter to the views of thoughtful analysts. Charles Kimball offers multiple examples of diverse religions becoming evil due to inflexible, absolutist, and exclusive truth claims, rigid dogma and doctrines, blind obedience, coercive pressure tactics, dire apocalyptic doctrines, emphasis on end times, good versus evil dichotomies, and violent conflicts over sacred space.[11] Martin Marty writes that the "killing dimension of religion is an interfaith

phenomenon. It's not only something that 'they' do, or something in 'their' scriptures."[12] Andrew Sullivan, although concerned about Islam and violence following the September 11, 2001, terrorist attacks, notes that most Muslims do not share bin Laden's views and that the "use of religion for extreme repression, and even terror, is not restricted to Islam. For most of its history Christianity has had a worse record."[13]

Sullivan, Kimball, and Marty stress the interfaith dimension of religious violence. They also note distinctive features that make monotheistic traditions prone to violence. Marty writes:

> Monotheists . . . have no monopoly on violence. But it is true that scripturally revealed monotheism can serve those minded to be lethal in distinctive ways. Believe in one all-powerful God. Believe that this God has enemies. Believe that you are charged to serve the purposes of God against those enemies. Believe that a unique and absolute holy book gives you directions, impulses, and motivations to prosecute war. You have then, the formula for crusades, holy wars, jihads, and . . . terrorism that knows no boundaries.[14]

IS GOD REALLY LIKE THIS?
OLD TESTAMENT IMAGES

There are many positive themes in the Bible, including love of God and neighbor, a deep desire to build a just social order, service, forgiveness, compassion, and hope. Violence, however, is easily the most prominent theme in the Bible and the dominant characteristic of God.[15] Humans are said to be created in God's image (Gen 1:26), and God announces that creation is very good (Gen 1:31). Unfortunately, God's violence dominates most of the story lines that follow. Explaining the flood to Noah God says, "I have determined to make an end of all flesh, for the earth is filled with violence because of them; now I am going to destroy them along with the earth" (Gen 6:13). We focus on arks and animals and take comfort in the postflood rainbow that symbolizes "an everlasting covenant between God and every living creature" (Gen 9:16). The rainbow was supposed to be a sign of God's promise to never be this destructive again, but God reneges: "I will utterly sweep away everything from the face of the earth, says the Lord" (Zeph 1:2).

Fear of God is an important biblical theme *and God often measures faith in relation to sufficient fear.* Abraham, poised to kill his son Isaac under direct orders from God, apparently received a last minute reprieve: "Do not lay your hand on the boy or do anything to him; for now I know that you fear God" (Gen 22:12). I say apparently because at various points in its history Israel practiced child sacrifice, and as one scholar notes, "in the original version of the story Isaac was actually sacrificed."[16] Conflicting views on child sacrifice may surprise some readers, but the Old Testament reflects the views of many different writers and draws on stories involving more than a thousand years of history. It is likely that the original story reflects a time in which child sacrifice was practiced in Israel as a way to appease or please God and that the story was edited in a later historical period when child sacrifice was no longer condoned.

Another common biblical theme is that *God proves to be God through demonstrative use of destructive violence.* Ezekiel sees punishing violence as God's defining signature. He uses the phrase (or variation of the same) "then you shall know that I am the Lord" at least sixty-five times. "Those far off shall die of pestilence; those nearby shall fall by the sword; and any who are left and are spared shall die of famine. Thus I will spend my fury upon them. And you shall know that I am the Lord" (Ezek 6:12–13a). "My anger shall spend itself, and I will vent my fury on them and satisfy myself; and they shall know that I, the Lord, have spoken in my jealousy, when I spend my fury on them" (Ezek 5:13).

God also sanctions murder of the disobedient. This practice reflects priestly preoccupations with holiness rooted in fear of God's punishing violence and how to avoid it. A man found gathering sticks on the Sabbath receives this harsh sentence: "And the Lord said to Moses, 'The man shall be put to death; all the congregation shall stone him outside the camp'" (Num 15:35). God also commands the community to stone to death rebellious sons in order "to purge the evil from your midst" (Deut 20:18–21). According to God's instructions to Moses, any children "who curse father or mother shall be put to death; having cursed father or mother, their blood is upon them" (Lev 20:9). If parents took this passage to heart, then we would all be dead. Lest we think that nobody pays attention to such ancient law codes, however, the principal justification for Christian hostility toward homosexuals is a verse found in the same chapter of Leviticus (20:13).

The desire to appease violent, unpredictable deities drives many biblical stories about offerings and sacrifices.[17] The "sacrifices of Cain and Abel suggest . . . an offering to ward off divine wrath," the Reform Jewish writer Regina Schwartz notes, "to encourage the deity's favor, to invoke his blessings of prosperity."[18] God accepts Abel's offering and rejects Cain's. The text doesn't say why. It leaves the distinct impression that God is violent, petty, arbitrary, and to be feared. The book of Acts reinforces these impressions in the story of Ananias and Sapphira. They sold their land and gave most of the proceeds to the faith community but were guilty of putting "the Spirit of the Lord to the test" (Acts 5:9) because they lied and kept part of the proceeds for themselves. Ananias "fell down and died. And great fear seized all who heard of it" (Acts 5:5). When boys called Elisha "baldhead," the insulted prophet cursed them "in the name of the Lord" and immediately two she-bears came out of the woods and mauled them (2 Kings 2:23–24).

Another aspect of troubling violence is described by Schwartz, who notes that "over and over the Bible tells the story of a people who inherit at someone else's expense."[19] *God, for example, is depicted as a determined and powerful land thief:*

> On that day the Lord made a covenant with Abram, saying, "To your descendants I give this land, from the river of Egypt to the great river, the river Euphrates, the land of the Kenites, the Kenizzites, the Kadmonites, the Hittites, the Perizzites, the Rephaim, the Amorites, the Canaanites, the Girgashites, and the Jebusites" (Gen 15:18–21).

We minimize the full weight of violence in this and similar passages by suggesting that God chose to give the land to the Israelites in order for Israel to be a blessing to all peoples. This is rarely what the Bible actually says, and it is an unconvincing argument given numerous passages that say otherwise. A disturbing story in Judges 11 links human sacrifice, land thievery, and God's violence. The Israelites take land from an Ammonite king who seeks peaceful redress. The king is told by Jephthah that the "Lord, the God of Israel, has conquered the Amorites for the benefit of

his people" who intend "to possess everything the Lord our God has conquered for our benefit" (Judg 11:23–24). Having appropriated the land by
divine fiat, Jephthah is determined to fight with God's help. He makes a
deal with God: Give "the Ammonites into my hand" and "whoever comes
out of the doors of my house to meet me, when I return victorious from
the Ammonites, shall be the Lord's, to be offered up by me as a burnt offering" (Judg 11:30–33a). Jephthah "inflicted a massive defeat on them"
(v. 33) and delivered his daughter up for slaughter (v. 39). When a male
warrior and a male deity plan together the result is often violence against
women.[20]

*The biblical writers often link God-ordained land thievery with divinely sanc-
tioned genocide.* "But the Lord said to Moses, 'Do not be afraid of him; for I
have given him into your hand, with all his people, and all his land.' . . . So
they killed him, his sons, and all his people, until there was no survivor
left; and they took possession of the land" (Num 21:31–35). "You must
utterly destroy them . . . show them no mercy" (Deut 7:2). We teach our
children the song "Joshua Fought the Battle of Jericho," but we leave out
the grisly scene that follows the collapse of the wall. "Then they devoted
to destruction by the edge of the sword all in the city, both men and
women, young and old, oxen, sheep, and donkeys" (Josh 6:19–21).

God deliberately hardened the hearts of groups inhabiting the land in
order to facilitate their extermination: "For it was the Lord's doing to
harden their hearts so that they would come against Israel in battle, in
order that they might be utterly destroyed, and might receive no mercy, but
be exterminated, just as the Lord had commanded Moses" (Josh 11:20).
Even more disturbing, God is said to have hardened Pharaoh's heart in
order to create an opportunity *to prove that God is God because of superior
violence.* "I will harden Pharaoh's heart, and he will pursue them, so that I
will gain glory for myself over Pharaoh and all his army; and the Egyptians
shall know that I am the Lord" (Exod 14:4).

*God, according to the book of Exodus, is willing and able to destroy Israel's
enemies with or without human agency.* "The hand of the Lord will strike
with a deadly pestilence" (9:3). "The Lord is a warrior; the Lord is his
name. Pharaoh's chariots and his army he cast into the sea; his picked

officers were sunk in the Red Sea" (Exod 15:3–4). "Thus says the Lord: About midnight I will go out through Egypt. Every firstborn in the land of Egypt shall die" (Exod 11:4). In this instance, God knew who and who not to kill because the Israelites had marked their doorposts and lintel with blood from the sacrifice of a lamb without blemish. This violent story gave rise to the Jewish celebration of Passover and to violent Christian interpretations of Jesus' death in sacrificial terms.

Regina M. Schwartz, like many other biblical scholars, notes that there is little or no evidence for the Exodus as history.[21] She points out, however, that the political and theological consequences of Exodus theology are enduring and devastating:

> And what about the biblical narrative? Should we hold it culpable for emblazoning this desire for land acquisition on its readers, inscribing deep into our culture the primordial myth of an Exodus that justifies conquest? From one perspective — that of history of the text — the conquest narrative is only a wild fantasy written by a powerless dispossessed people who dream of wondrous victories over their enemies, of living in a land where milk and honey flow, and of entering that land with the blessing and support of an Almighty Deity. But from another perspective — that of the text's political afterlife — there is another story that is less appealing and considerably less innocent, telling of creating a people through the massive displacement and destruction of other peoples, of laying claim to a land that had belonged to others, and of conducting this bloody conquest under the banner of divine will.[22]

Biblical stories can become critical building blocks for contemporary politics and violence. For example, exodus stories are cited frequently by fundamentalist Christians today to justify their support for brutal Israeli policies against Palestinians and by Jewish groups to justify expansion of settlements onto Palestinian land.

The many punishments that disobedient Israelites receive from God's hand are another manifestation of the Bible's unrelenting violence. Here is a sampling from a vast body of biblical material:

I myself will fight against you with outstretched hand and mighty arm, in anger, in fury, and in great wrath. And I will strike down the inhabitants of this city, both human beings and animals; they shall die of a great pestilence. (Jer 21:5–6)

See, the day of the Lord comes, cruel, with wrath and fierce anger, to make the earth a desolation, and to destroy its sinners from it. . . . Whoever is found will be thrust through, and whoever is caught will fall by the sword. Their infants will be dashed to pieces before their eyes; their houses will be plundered, and their wives ravished. See, I am stirring up the Medes against them. (Isa 13:9, 15–17a)

The hands of compassionate women have boiled their own children; they became their food in the destruction of my people. The Lord gave full vent to his wrath; he poured out his hot anger, and kindled a fire in Zion that consumed its foundations. (Lam 4:10–11)

This brief survey of violent images of God in the Hebrew scriptures raises troubling issues. Christians, however, frequently downplay them by associating them with the Old Testament. Unfortunately, violent themes and violent expectations of God also permeate the New Testament.

IS GOD REALLY LIKE THIS?
NEW TESTAMENT IMAGES

Violent images and expectations of God dominate the New Testament and are in continuity with violence in the Hebrew scriptures. Mary's song (Luke 1:46–53) parallels verse by verse that of Hannah (1 Sam 2:1–5). Each celebrates or anticipates a historical reversal rooted in God's violence in which enemies are defeated, the rich are displaced, and the poor are exalted. John the Baptist neatly divides the world between good and evil (wheat and chaff). His God is wrathful and fully capable of punitive violence. John tells the "brood of vipers" that come to him in the wilderness that God's violent coming is imminent and warns that the chaff will soon be burned "with unquenchable fire" (Luke 3:7–12).

The author of Revelation embraces the violent images of God common to the Baptist and the Hebrew scriptures. Anyone who argues that violent images of God are confined to the Old Testament should consider passages such as these from Revelation:

> Sovereign Lord, holy and true, how long will it be before you judge and avenge our blood on the inhabitants of the earth? (6:10)

> So the four angels were released, who had been held ready for the hour, the day, the month, and the year, to kill a third of humankind. (9:13–15)

> We give you thanks, Lord God Almighty, who are and who were, for you have taken your great power and begun to reign. The nations raged, but your wrath has come, and the time for judging the dead, for rewarding your servants, the prophets and saints and all who fear your name, both small and great, and for destroying those who destroy the earth. (11:17–18)

New Testament violence is not limited to the apocalyptic views of John the Baptist and the author of Revelation. At times Matthew's Jesus[23] sounds exactly like John the Baptist. "Every tree that does not bear good fruit is cut down and thrown into the fire" (Matt 7:19). "You snakes, you brood of vipers! How can you escape being sentenced to hell?" (Matt 23:33). Key actors in the oppressive system of first-century Palestine are exposed in Jesus' parables only to be treated as "God figures" by Matthew, who blesses their violence with the authority of Jesus' voice.[24] These "God figures" consistently send people to the torturers or to other terrible punishments.

One of the favorite activities of Matthew's Jesus is to threaten people with violent punishments using his preferred phrase, "weeping and gnashing of teeth." "Then the king said to the attendants, 'Bind him hand and foot, and throw him into the outer darkness, where there will be weeping and gnashing of teeth'" (Matt 22:13). Then "the master of that slave will come on a day when he does not expect him and at an hour that he does not know. He will cut him in pieces and put him with the hypocrites, where there will be weeping and gnashing of teeth" (Matt 24:50–51). "But his master replied, 'You wicked and lazy slave.... As for this worthless slave, throw him into

the outer darkness, where there will be weeping and gnashing of teeth'"
(Matt 25:26a, 30). More familiar to many of us is the violent ending to the
great judgment parable in Matthew 25:31–46, in which Matthew's Jesus
sends those who don't feed the hungry into "eternal punishment" (v 46).

WHY ALL THE VIOLENCE?

The violent images and expectations of God described above are the tip
of a very large iceberg. Pervasive violence visible at the tip tells us that
violence is a serious issue, but it doesn't tell us why it's there or help us see
whether and how Christian theology, worship, music, and liturgies have
been shaped consciously or unconsciously by violent images of God. We
can better answer the question, "Why all the violence?" if we remember
that the tip of an iceberg rests on a broad foundation. When we look at the
foundation we see that nearly all the violence visible at the tip is connected
to the three most important *theological* story lines in the Bible. Theology,
according to my definition, is any effort to make sense out of our lives and
what is happening in our world in relation to God, Spirit, or the Divine.
By this definition the biblical writers are theologians, and so are we. They
made sense out of their lives, history, and God in the context of three key
biblical story lines: Exodus, Exile, and the Apocalyptic worldview. Violent
images of God are at the center of each.

EXODUS: LIBERATING VIOLENCE

Exodus is perhaps the central motif in the Bible. Apart from the Exodus story we cannot comprehend the mixture of pride, pain, expectation,
disappointment, fear, hope, rage, despair, and confusion evident in many
texts. In Exodus theology the Exodus is interpreted as a story of *God's
liberating violence*. God proves to be God through superior violence that
defeats enemies. Projecting violent power onto God was and is an alluring
fantasy. In its idealized place in the tradition, Exodus theology describes
a liberating God who is powerful and ethnically partial. God hears the
cries of an oppressed people, knows their sufferings, and identifies with
their plight.[25] God authorizes the chosen people to take control of a good

land even though powerful Egyptians block their way and the "Promised Land" is inhabited by others. The liberating God of Exodus theology frees the Israelites by defeating their Egyptian oppressors and helps them seek control of the land through genocidal violence.

EXILE: PUNISHING VIOLENCE

Exile theology responded to the fact that history rarely if ever conformed to the promises and expectations of the Exodus. Instead of dominating others and living securely in the land under the divine protection of a God of superior violence, the Israelites lost control of the land and were scattered throughout the nations after being crushed and dominated by one empire after another. Exile theology is the product of priestly and prophetic writers who explain with brutal simplicity the contradiction between Exodus expectations and exilic reality. The chosen people are exiled because they deserve it. At the heart of Exile theology is the *punishing violence of God.* I could cite literally hundreds of biblical passages to illustrate the exilic story line of God's punishing violence but I will limit myself to one from the book of Leviticus:

> If you follow my statutes and keep my commandments and observe them faithfully, I will give you your rains in their season, and the land shall yield its produce, and the trees of the field shall yield their fruit...; you shall eat your bread to the full, and live securely in your land. And I will grant peace in the land.... You shall give chase to your enemies, and they shall fall before you by the sword.... But if you will not obey me, and do not observe all these commandments...I in turn will do this to you. I will bring terror on you; consumption and fever that waste the eyes and cause life to pine away. You shall sow your seed in vain, for your enemies shall eat it. I will set my face against you, and you shall be struck down by your enemies.... And if in spite of this you will not obey me, I will continue to punish you sevenfold for your sins...I will bring the sword against you, executing vengeance for the covenant; and if you withdraw within your cities, I will send pestilence among you,

GOD PUNISHES SIN

and you shall be delivered into enemy hands. . . . You shall eat the flesh of your sons, and you shall eat the flesh of your daughters. I will destroy your high places and cut down your incense altars; I will heap your carcasses on the carcasses of your idols. I will abhor you. I will lay your cities waste, will make your sanctuaries desolate, and I will not smell your pleasing odors. I will devastate the land, so that your enemies who come to settle in it shall be appalled at it. And you I will scatter among the nations, and I will unsheathe the sword against you; your land shall be a desolation, and your cities a waste.
(Lev 26:3–7, 14–18, 24b–33).

There are three other important things to note about Exile theology. First, the Leviticus text and many others like it were written in the context of exile. In other words, *bad historical experiences preceded this theology.* Theologians in exile offered this theology in order to explain and justify what had already happened. In an effort to maintain the integrity of God, they wrote that God had warned the people that bad conduct would result in historical catastrophes and then inserted these warnings into early parts of the tradition.

Second, these same theologians living in exile transformed the Jewish God (Yahweh) from that of a regional, tribal deity into *the* universal and all-powerful God. They reconciled the huge discrepancies between Exodus expectations and Exile realities by declaring that Israel's God was responsible for everything that happened in history. This included Israel's destruction at the hand of foreign empires, which they interpreted as God's punishment for disobedience or sin.

Finally, prophets also crafted Exile theology but they often coupled announcements of God's terrifying judgment with *promises of a glorious reversal.* Israel was presently being punished for its many failings, but God's liberating violence would one day allow Israel to oppress their oppressors. This theme of reversal is so central to the Hebrew scriptures that *salvation came to mean defeat of enemies* (Exod 14:30, 15:1–4; Ps 18:45–48). Isaiah writes:

> It will be said on that day, Lo, this is our God; we have waited for him, so that he might *save us.* This is the Lord for whom we have waited; let us be glad and rejoice in his *salvation.* For the hand of the Lord will rest on this mountain. The Moabites shall be trodden down in their place as straw is trodden down in a dung-pit.
>
> (Isa 25:9–10, emphasis added)

> Thus says the Lord God: I will soon lift up my hand to the nations, and raise my signal to the peoples; and they shall bring your sons in their bosom, and your daughters shall be carried on their shoulders. Kings shall be your foster fathers, and their queens your nursing mothers. With their faces to the ground they shall bow down to you, and lick the dust off your feet. Then you will know that I am the Lord; those who wait for me shall not be put to shame...for I will contend with those who contend with you, and I will save your children. I will make your oppressors eat their own flesh, and they shall be drunk with their own blood as with wine. Then all flesh shall know that I am the Lord your Savior, and your Redeemer, the Mighty One of Jacob. (Isa 49:22–23, 25b–26)

> Foreigners shall build up your walls, and their kings shall minister to you; for in my wrath I struck you down, but in my favor I have had

mercy on you. Your gates shall always be open; day and night they shall not be shut, so that nations shall bring you their wealth, with their kings led in procession. For the nation and kingdom that will not serve you shall perish; those nations shall be utterly laid waste.

(Isa 60:10–12)

APOCALYPTIC THEOLOGY: VINDICATING VIOLENCE

The apocalyptic worldview, the third major biblical story line, emerged after centuries passed in which the promised, glorious historical reversal never materialized. Although Exile theology and the apocalyptic worldview embrace images of a punishing God, apocalypticism is utterly pessimistic about history. Isaiah had promised a glorious reversal of fortune within history. The apocalyptic worldview placed hope in an imminent violent coming of God to end the world as we know it. The priests and prophets had explained terrible historical tragedies as a consequence of Israel's sin and disobedience that resulted in God's punishing violence. The apocalyptic writers and prophets explained the nation's plight in relation to a cosmic struggle between good and evil. God didn't want the people to be dominated by foreign empires, but God was preoccupied with a cosmic war against the forces of evil in heaven. The bad news was that until God won the cosmic battle the people on earth would be oppressed. The good news was that God was winning and would soon judge the world with unfathomable violence. The faithful would be vindicated and rise to eternal life, and those who were evil would be defeated and sentenced to permanent hell.

Apocalyptic theology is featured prominently in the books of Daniel and Revelation. It is embraced by John the Baptist and the apostle Paul and it becomes a principal lens through which the Gospel writers interpret the meaning of Jesus' life and death. Apocalyptic theology was another attempt to maintain God's credibility in light of failed promises by explaining historical catastrophes in a new light.

CONCLUSION

Jesus and his contemporaries were socialized into Exodus, Exile, and Apoc-alyptic theologies rooted in violent images of God. Given the high degree of violence within these story lines it isn't surprising that violent expec-tations of God carry over into the New Testament and spill over into traditional Christian theology, worship, music, and liturgies. Jesus lives under an oppressive Roman dominated system. He challenges Rome's abusive power and many of the violent images of God and expectations of history that are at the heart of the key story lines of his tradition.

DISCUSSION

Our Focus: To clearly name the uncomfortable facts facing us concerning violent images of God.

Discuss one or more of the questions in each of the four categories.

Objective Questions

1. What was new information (or a new idea) for you in this chapter?

2. What words or phrases stand out for you after reading this chapter?

3. What are some of the troubling images that the author finds in reading through the Bible?

Reflective Questions

4. Describe your feelings when biblical passages cited in chapter 1 are read.

5. How does it feel to have someone speak up and question or challenge biblical violence? (not do you agree, but what feelings do you have?)

6. Did you read here anything you have long felt and wanted to say?

7. Were you angered by any of this? Which part? Why?

Interpretive Questions

8. Do we downplay biblical violence in our congregation? If so, how?

9. What effect does this violence in scripture have on our congregation's life right now? Do we see it? If so, where?

10. What time-honored beliefs of yours (or this congregation's) are being challenged in this chapter?

11. How do you view the authority of the Bible? How does this compare with the author's view?

12. Do the biblical passages cited in the chapter reflect the God of your experience?

13. What do you think God's power is like?

Decisional Questions

14. What title would you like to give this chapter? (Be creative)

15. Where (or how) might we use this information so that it has positive value for us?

ACTIVITY

Bible Verses on Cards

Collect eight or ten Bible verses referred to in chapter 1, and write each on a separate card. Proceed with one of the following options:

Option 1. Does This Fit? Divide into small groups. Give each group one card to discuss and then to rank on a scale from one to ten (one being "this fits totally with my faith today," and ten being "I don't believe in this god.") Allow five minutes, and then have groups read their cards aloud and explain their decision.

Option 2. Standing on a Continuum. Read the collected Bible passages one at a time. After each passage is read, invite folks to position themselves along a continuum (an imaginary line spanning the room). Designate one wall as "This fits totally with my faith today" and the opposite wall as "I don't believe in this god." The center of the room would be "can't decide" or "50/50."

Draw a Cartoon

Choose one of the issues raised by the author in this chapter and develop a cartoon showing the crux of the matter for you personally.

NOTES

1. For a fictional account of the war against progressive religious in Latin America see Jack Nelson-Pallmeyer, *Harvest of Cain* (Washington, D.C.: EPICA, 2001). For a non-fiction account of this war see Jack Nelson-Pallmeyer, *School of Assassins: Guns, Greed, and Globalization* (Maryknoll, N.Y.: Orbis Books, 2001).

2. Jack Nelson-Pallmeyer, *Is Religion Killing Us? Violence in the Bible and the Quran* (Harrisburg, Pa.: Trinity Press International, 2003).

3. Andrew Sullivan, "This Is a Religious War," *New York Times Magazine*, October 7, 2001, 45.

4. Nelson-Pallmeyer, *Is Religion Killing Us?* chapter 1.

5. Sullivan, "This Is a Religious War," 45–46.

6. Martha Sawyer Allen, "Religion as Significant Factor in War," *Star Tribune* (December 28, 2003).

7. Ibid.

8. In *Is Religion Killing Us?* I describe violence of God traditions at the heart of the Bible and the Quran, including many dozens of passages from the Quran that could be reasonably interpreted to justify violence in defense of faith or in pursuit of justice. See especially chapter 6.

9. See Jack Nelson-Pallmeyer, *School of Assassins: Guns, Greed, and Globalization* (Maryknoll, N.Y.: Orbis Books, 2001).

10. Except as otherwise noted all Bible quotes are from *The New Oxford Annotated Bible: New Revised Standard Version with the Apocrypha* (Oxford: Oxford University Press, 2001).

11. Charles Kimball, *When Religion Becomes Evil* (San Francisco: HarperSanFrancisco, 2002).

12. Martin E. Marty, "Is Religion the Problem?" *Tikkun* (March–April 2002).

13. Sullivan, "This Is a Religious War," 45.

14. Marty, "Is Religion the Problem?"

15. See Jack Nelson-Pallmeyer, *Jesus against Christianity: Reclaiming the Missing Jesus* (Harrisburg, Pa.: Trinity Press International, 2001), chaps. 1–5. See also Nelson-Pallmeyer, *Is Religion Killing Us?* 132, in which I argue that "Jews, Christians, and Muslims do reasonably well in terms of compassionate, just, ethical, and moral living . . . *in spite of much of what is in their 'sacred' texts.*"

16. Richard Elliott Friedman, *Who Wrote the Bible?* (San Francisco: HarperSanFrancisco, 1987), 257.

17. I speak about deities rather than Deity to make the point that although we associate the Bible with monotheism the priestly writers throughout most of Israel's history assumed there were many gods. They disagreed with each other over the proper names for god, the characteristics of god, and what sacrifices were pleasing to god. In competition with other god claims, they made the case that their god was superior to other gods, not that their god was the only god. Superior violence often defined superiority. The monotheistic idea of one God emerged late in the tradition, probably during the Babylonian captivity (after 587 B.C.E.). At that time, editors imposed a monotheistic overlay over earlier biblical materials that were part of a polytheistic tradition. They also grafted most of the powers and characteristics of neighboring gods onto one, all-powerful Deity. See Nelson-Pallmeyer, *Jesus against Christianity,* chapters 6–7.

18. Regina M. Schwartz, *The Curse of Cain: The Violent Legacy of Monotheism* (Chicago: University of Chicago Press, 1997), 68.

19. Ibid., x.

20. Nelson-Pallmeyer, *Jesus against Christianity,* 30.

21. A core issue related to an honest look at biblical violence is what authority we are to give scripture. Some Christians are literalists who embrace the Bible as God's word. Others see the Bible as written by humans but divinely inspired. We see the biblical writers as human theologians who offer their views about God in the context of their lives. Many of their views portray God and Jesus in irreconcilable ways. We have no good choice but to sift through their competing portraits in light of our own experience and our understanding of Jesus. Our approach to the Bible is evident in chapters 3 and 4.

22. Schwartz, *The Curse of Cain,* 57.

23. Each Gospel offers different and irreconcilable portraits of Jesus. Jesus is pitted against Jesus within each book itself and between the different Gospels. I refer to Matthew's Jesus to indicate that Matthew's portrait of Jesus differs from that of Mark and Luke and John, and it often differs from Jesus himself. Matthew's theology portrays Jesus in an apocalyptic light, but Matthew also presents evidence that the historical Jesus rejected apocalyptic views and expectations. See chapters 2 and 3.

24. See William R. Herzog II, *Parables as Subversive Speech: Jesus as Pedagogue of the Oppressed* (Louisville: Westminster/John Knox Press, 1994).

25. For a critique of this idealized version see Nelson-Pallmeyer, *Jesus against Christianity,* chapter 4.

CHAPTER 2

JESUS' SOCIAL SETTING

The focus of the present chapter is on the social world of Jesus. I briefly describe Roman imperial rule, the plight of the people, the complicity of the Temple in the oppressive social order, and how Jesus' contemporaries understood the crisis, including what they expected from God and history. Seeing Jesus in his social world helps us understand his radical challenge to his tradition, including his rejection of violent images of God, his call to love enemies, and his embrace of nonviolence.

THREE PILLARS OF ROME'S IMPERIAL SYSTEM

Jesus was a radical Palestinian Jew who lived in first-century, Rome-occupied Palestine. Rome's power touched all aspects of life. Its system of taxes, tribute, and commercialization of land impoverished many peasants. Its arrogance included religious claims concerning the blessings of the gods and the divinity of the emperor. Its brutality featured massacres and crucifixions of potential and actual rebels as part of a strategy of psychological warfare, intimidation, and control. Its propaganda and ideological persuasion included promotion of the emperor cult and Rome's "Gospel" of peace through military conquest.

Roman imperial rule was brutally efficient. It rested on three pillars. First, Rome appointed local client kings to govern on its behalf. These client kings carried out imperial policies well or they were replaced. The second pillar was the Temple. The Roman imperial system could not function smoothly in Palestine without cooperation and cooptation of religious officials connected to the Temple, an institution of enormous political, economic, and religious consequence in first-century Palestine. Roman governors and client kings exercised ultimate authority over the Temple.

The high priest, a political appointee of the Roman empire, had little choice but to serve Roman interests. One symbol of his dependency is that the sacred vestments (worn by the high priest when he entered the Holy of Holies, the most sacred space within the Temple, on the Day of Atonement, the holiest day of the year) were kept in Roman hands and released to the high priest on condition of pleasing Rome.

Jewish priestly leaders were important enough to be given a stake in the oppressive system. The high priests who benefited from collaborative rule influenced society directly and through retainers such as the scribes and Pharisees. They collected taxes and tribute and helped maintain order on behalf of Rome. As Richard Horsley notes, the high priests "were saddled with the responsibility of maintaining order in Jerusalem. Roman officials could — and did — appoint them and depose them at will."[1]

The third pillar of the oppressive system was Roman military power. Legions of Roman soldiers were ready if called upon to crush any and all opposition when client kings or Temple elites failed in carrying out their appointed duties. The "Roman response to such a situation was massive military action and the crucifixion of all common people who had taken part, and a rendering of accounts from the respective aristocracies."[2]

DEPRESSING TIMES

The historical setting into which Jesus was born was particularly depressing. Jesus' birth corresponded roughly to the death of Herod the Great, Rome's most efficient, brutal, and cunning client king. Herod's death prompted hope and rebellion throughout Palestine. Messianic expectations, already running high in preceding decades, had risen to a fever pitch. The time for Israel's liberation with the help of God's redeeming violence seemed to have arrived. Many Jews, apparently inspired by the liberating violence of God tradition, fought the Roman soldiers expecting a military savior to free Israel and crush Rome.[3] The rebellions started well and ended badly. Jewish fighters took over a Roman arsenal, and the people appointed their own popular kings and messiahs to rule over them. Isaiah's vision of Israel's triumph over the nations seemed ready for completion by God. Roman legions later defeated the insurgencies, slaughtered Jews, and burned cities, including the major urban center in Galilee (Sepphoris) that was only four miles from Jesus' hometown of Nazareth. Roman soldiers lined the roads with thousands of corpse-filled crosses. Decaying flesh served as food for birds and wild animals and as public deterrent to survivors.

The defeat of popular kings and messiahs had devastating implications beyond the carnage of war. It marked another failure of historical promise and theological vision. Rome's triumph discredited prophetic promises that God's liberating violence would *save* Israel and accomplish a glorious reversal of Israel's destiny *within history*. It set the stage for John the Baptist's historically pessimistic apocalyptic promises that God's punishing violence would soon *vindicate* the faithful *at the end of history*. Those who experienced crushing historical defeats found hope in apocalyptic promises that soon apocalyptic violence at the end time would avenge historical injustices. Historical setbacks and apocalyptic promises also help to explain why the Gospel writers used heavily apocalyptic language and themes to explain the death of Jesus, the death of yet another messiah.

We meet Jesus in the Gospels as an adult living under an oppressive social order imposed by Rome. The area of Judah, which included Jerusalem, was at the time under direct Roman rule with Pilate in charge because one of Herod's sons hadn't properly maintained order. Jesus' home province of Galilee, where many of the stories and parables of Jesus are set, was administered by Antipas, another of Herod's sons. The oppressive system that was governed and secured by Rome-appointed rulers, Temple elites, and Roman legions benefited a select few but impoverished the vast majority of Jesus' contemporaries.

John Dominic Crossan describes an "abysmal gulf separating the upper from the lower classes." On one side were rulers and governors who together made up 1 percent of the population and owned at least half of the land; priests, who owned as much as 15 percent of the land; retainers (military generals and expert bureaucrats); and merchants. The other side consisted of peasants — "that vast majority of the population about two-thirds of whose annual crop went to support the upper classes"; the artisans, who were below the peasants in social class and made up about

5 percent of the population; and the expendables, about "10 percent of the population, ranging from beggars and outlaws to hustlers, day laborers, and slaves." "If Jesus was a carpenter . . . ," Crossan writes, "he belonged to the Artisan class, that group pushed into the dangerous space between Peasants and . . . Expendables."[4]

RELIGIOUS COMPLICITY WITH INJUSTICE

Jesus clashed frequently with religious officials and the Temple because they shored up the oppressive system. Temple elites, including high priestly families, collaborated with the Romans in collecting tribute and taxes that often led to peasant indebtedness and forced eviction from their land. As Richard Horsley notes, the "Temple was clearly the basis of an economic system in which the agricultural producers supported the priests, particularly the priestly aristocracy who administered the system and were its chief beneficiaries."[5] Peasants were crushed under the weight of double taxation. They paid tribute and taxes to the Romans under the threat of military reprisals and tithes to the Temple under the combined threat of sacred obligations, threatened violence, and fear of religious ostracism. Religious taxes were collected forcibly, if necessary, by Pharisees and other religious functionaries. Horsley writes:

> Villagers of Galilee (like all other members of the People of Israel) were instructed to set aside a significant portion of their produce for priestly tithes, first-fruits offerings, and various other sacred dona-tions for the Temple in Jerusalem [in addition to the royal taxes]. By the first century, every Israelite male was required to make an annual contribution of a half-shekel to the Temple (and for villagers, that coin could be obtained only through the exchange of crops or agri-cultural products — in addition to the ten percent already required for the annual tithe). And even in seasons when drought or blight severely limited the harvest, the tax collectors and priestly represen-tatives still turned up at the local threshing floors and olive presses to make sure that every family contributed their due. Penalties for

nonpayment could be severe and violent when the farmers of a particular village or region did not willingly yield up the lion's share of their harvest to satisfy the demands of the official representatives of the Jerusalem Temple and Herodian state.[6]

Archeological evidence demonstrates that collaboration with Rome benefited high priestly families. They "amassed considerable fortunes" and lived "elegant" lifestyles in spacious mansions with "mosaic-floored reception rooms and dining rooms with elaborate painted and carved stucco wall decoration and with a wealth of fine tableware, glassware, carved stone tabletops and other interior furnishings."[7]

COMPETING PORTRAITS OF JESUS

Discerning how Jesus responded to his social world is difficult because the Gospels present not a single portrait of Jesus but rather numerous, incompatible, irreconcilable portraits. The Gospels, in other words, pit Jesus against Jesus. For example, Jesus is portrayed as both embracing and rejecting the apocalyptic worldview. Drawing on Gospel stories, I can make a rather convincing case that Jesus is apocalyptic, that he shares many of John the Baptist's views concerning the imminent violent coming of God, and that he fully expects the world to end in his lifetime. I can also make what I think is a more compelling case that Jesus isn't apocalyptic, that he rejects many of John's views, that he is concerned about the imminence of God here and now, that he rejects messianic and apocalyptic fantasies of freedom through God's violence, and that he embraces nonviolence. Both portraits can't be true.[8]

The Gospels also pit Jesus against Christ. One common and somewhat helpful explanation for many contradictory portraits of Jesus is that the Gospels contain stories of the historical Jesus *and* interpretations of Jesus as the Christ rooted in the beliefs of early Christian communities. This explanation says we have evidence of the pre-Easter Jesus, a real historical person, and evidence of the post-Easter Jesus or Christ of faith that reflects the beliefs of those communities that experienced the crucified and resurrected Jesus as their Savior. This division, although true to a point, doesn't

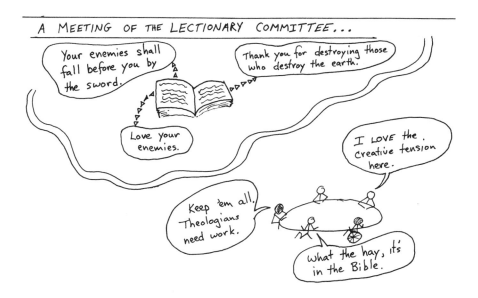

help us with the central problem, namely, that the images of God central to the nonviolent stream of Jesus often clash sharply with the images of God at the heart of New Testament interpretations of Jesus as the Christ. Jesus rejects the apocalyptic worldview only to have the Gospel writers interpret the meaning of his life and death in an apocalyptic light.

As I have written elsewhere, we have no good choice but to choose between irreconcilable portraits of Jesus and God found within the Bible.[9] I'm not going to repeat that case here. I want to remind readers, however, that central to these conflicts over competing biblical portrayals of God and Jesus and differences between the Jesus of history and the Christ of faith are radically different conceptions of God's power and important issues concerning violence and nonviolence. These conflicts and differences have profound implications for Christian theology, worship, and action. The Gospel writers provide evidence that Jesus embraces nonviolence and a radically different view of God's power. They, and much of traditional Christianity, however, largely reject this nonviolent stream. They rely on the violent stories and traditions described in chapter 1 to interpret the meaning of Jesus' life and death, to convey images of God, and to frame Christian theology, worship, music, and liturgies.

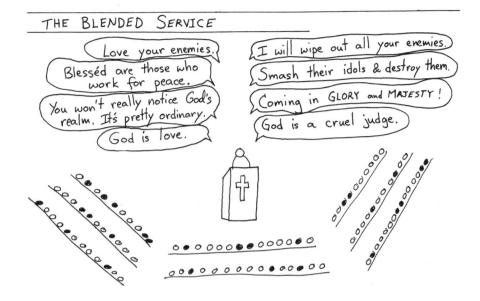

COMMON RESPONSES TO OCCUPATION

Jewish groups on the scene shortly before, during, or closely following Jesus' crucifixion offered diverse explanations or responses to historical calamities in first-century Palestine. The Sadducees seemed to collaborate most willingly with Rome. Most others resisted in one form or another. Richard Horsley notes that Rome's "repressive tolerance" of religion led groups like the Pharisees away from exercise of faith in a "social-political" way and to focus instead "on personal piety and purity in their brotherhoods." This reinforced "the focus on sin as the cause of individual and collective suffering."[10] In this light, foreign domination of Israel was understood to be God's punishment for the people's lack of personal piety and holiness that made the nation unholy. Presumably, greater personal piety and holiness would trigger God's favor, possibly including God's redemptive violence and action, to free Israel and defeat Rome.

Apocalyptic prophets like John the Baptist and groups like the Essenes hated both the Romans and their Jewish collaborators. They were outraged by the enduring oppression but pessimistic about the possibility of justice within history. They looked toward a final, end-time battle between the forces of good and evil and to a final judgment that was imminent. The Essenes, and perhaps John as well, understood the people's historical defeat and Rome's brutal occupation as God's punishment because illegitimate priests ran the Jerusalem Temple in ways that undermined the possibility of a just religious, political, social order.

The apocalyptic Essenes had fled into the desert after a rival priestly faction took control of the Jewish Temple more than 150 years before the birth of Jesus. They could not imagine resolving their differences with others within society or within history. They withdrew and lived with disciplined and pious fervor in anticipation of a new violent coming of God, at which time the present leaders of the polluted Temple would be destroyed. After Rome occupied Israel, they adjusted their vision anticipating that God's judgment would be against both Pagan Rome and its illegitimate religious collaborators.

Hatred of enemies was a core tenet of the Essenes. They taught that the "man of understanding" is expected to "hate all that He [God] has despised." Members of their community were to "love all the sons of light" and "hate the sons of darkness" each "according to his fault in the Vengeance of God." "These are the norms of conduct for the man of understanding in these times, concerning what he must love and how he must hate," the *Rule of the Community* states: "Everlasting hatred for all men of the pit because of their spirit of hoarding."[11] The *War Scroll* of the Essenes is described by Uta Ranke-Heinemann:

> This hatred will break out in the approaching eschatological war. The end of the world, which the Qumran sect expected to come soon, would be preceded by a war of revenge and retribution, the war of the "sons of light" (the Qumran community) against the "sons of darkness." This war is described in detail in the *War Scroll* (1 QM).... It will go on for forty years. In the first twenty years, all the foreign nations will be conquered; in the following twenty, all other Jews.[12]

Other Jewish groups used terrorism and violence to resist Roman occupation. Unorganized social banditry was widespread, and organized groups like the Sicarii and Zealots attacked Jewish collaborators and Roman occupiers directly rather than wait for the apocalyptic violence of God. The

Sicarii were daggermen who went about Jerusalem assassinating Jewish leaders who collaborated with the Romans. The most organized violent rebellion was that of the Zealots who fought the Romans during the Jewish revolt of 66–70 C.E.

QUESTIONS AND ANSWERS OLD AND NEW

Jews in first-century Palestine would have asked themselves two fundamental questions in the context of Roman occupation and in light of the three violent story lines that dominated the tradition. "How did we displease God?" The presumption is that an all-powerful God controlled everything that happened. Historical catastrophes, including Roman occupation, were interpreted in the context of God's punishing violence. A second question would have been, "What can we do to trigger God's favor?" The presumption in this case is that changes in the people's behavior could trigger either God's liberating violence to free them from Rome or God's apocalyptic violence to vindicate them and crush their evil enemies for all time at the end of history. Jesus in contrast to these explanations and expectations places little emphasis on the prominent Jewish theme of national repentance as a means to escape punishment from God's judgment.[13] This is because, as Crossan notes, "Jesus did *not* think imperial oppression was a divine punishment. It was simply an injustice that the Jews and God would have to resist as best they could. Jesus, and probably most peasants, knew exactly where the fault lay, and they did not blame on Jewish sin what came rather from Roman greed."[14]

CONCLUSION

This brief introduction into Jesus' social world indicates that he lived within an oppressive system imposed by Rome in which Jewish religious leaders were complicit and the vast majority of people impoverished. Jesus and his contemporaries were socialized Jews who tried to make sense out of their historical plight and future possibilities in relation to God and the three dominant story lines described in the previous chapters. They groped for explanations and for reasons to hope. Was oppression punishment from

God? What could they do to encourage God's liberating violence and to hold back God's punishing violence? Would God's liberating violence eventually free them? Or should they embrace apocalyptic expectations? Should they prepare for God's vindicating violence that would end the world as they knew it and give them permanent salvation and the satisfaction of watching their enemies fry? Or were there other ways to make sense of their plight and other forms of resistance? We have seen how many of Jesus' contemporaries answered these questions. As Christians, we must try to discern how Jesus and the Gospel writers answered them. What did Jesus say and do and how did he encourage others to live in the midst of the oppressive social setting described above? How did he understand God and God's power in this context? How did he define what it meant to live an authentic, faithful life?

DISCUSSION

Our Focus: To become familiar with the difficult times in which Jesus lived.

Discuss one or more of the questions in each of the four categories.

Objective Questions

1. What pictures of Jesus' life and times do we get from this chapter?

2. What struck you about first-century Palestine? What was Roman rule like? What was Jesus up against?

3. What contradictory images of Jesus and God in the Bible are named by the author? What contradictory images of Jesus and God do you find in the Bible?

Reflective Questions

4. Where in this chapter did you really sit up and take notice?

5. What associations crossed your mind as you were reading?

6. What parts of this chapter did you have trouble understanding?

7. What did you like or not like about this chapter?

Interpretive Questions

8. In the ancient world, most people thought the crushing difficulties of life were God's punishment for sin. What do you believe?

9. What parts of this chapter are you struggling with? Excited about?

10. The Jews in first-century Palestine felt powerless and depressed. What parts of today's reality make you feel that way? How does that shape your understanding of God?

11. What are your thoughts about the cartoon "The Bible's Not Relevant" (on page 14)?

12. Where in today's world would there be people who could relate to problems such as those faced by Jesus and the people in first-century Palestine?

Decisional Questions

13. The author points out that in some places the Bible says one thing and in others something quite different. How do you resolve for yourself conflicting messages within the Bible?

14. What can we do with this information about the times of Jesus' life?

15. What parts of this historical information (if any) would you like to include in our church's educational curriculum? How should we proceed on that?

ACTIVITY

Add Dialog to a Cartoon

Make copies of the cartoon "The Bible's Not Relevant" (on page 14). Divide into small groups. Invite each group to discuss the cartoon and then add dialog. They can simply draw a bubble from one or more of the people shown and add words they think the people are saying. Groups can have multiple copies and come up with more than one "take" on the words being said by the people. Allow 10 minutes and then have groups share their results.

NOTES

1. Richard Horsley and Neil Asher Silberman, *The Message and the Kingdom* (New York: Grosset/Putman, 1997), 79. See also John Dominic Crossan, *Jesus: A Revolutionary Biography* (New York: HarperCollins, 1995), 136.

2. Richard Horsley, *Jesus and the Spiral of Violence: Popular Jewish Resistance in Roman Palestine* (Minneapolis: Fortress Press, 1993), 32.

3. Horsley and Silberman, *The Message and the Kingdom,* 14–15.

4. Crossan, *Jesus: A Revolutionary Biography,* 25–26.

5. Horsley, *Jesus and the Spiral of Violence,* 286.

6. Horsley and Silberman, *The Message and the Kingdom,* 28.

7. Ibid., 78–79.

8. My own view is that Jesus was initially a follower of John the Baptist who broke with John because Jesus' images of God and his expectations of history differed profoundly from those of John. If Jesus was at one time John's disciple this might explain some of the apocalyptic sentiments attributed to him in the Gospels. The case that Jesus isn't apocalyptic, however, is so strong that I think it likely that the apocalyptic ideas of the Gospel writers themselves were imposed onto Jesus.

9. Jack Nelson-Pallmeyer, *Jesus against Christianity: Reclaiming the Missing Jesus* (Harrisburg, Pa.: Trinity Press International, 2001).

10. Horsley, *Jesus and the Spiral of Violence,* 45.

11. Uta Ranke-Heinemann, *Putting Away Childish Things* (San Francisco: HarperSanFrancisco, 1995), 259.

12. Ibid.

13. See John Dominic Crossan, *The Birth of Christianity* (San Francisco: HarperSanFrancisco, 1998), 339.

14. Ibid., emphasis in original.

CHAPTER 3

JESUS BREAKS NEW NONVIOLENT GROUND IN TEN CORE BIBLE PASSAGES

The focus of this chapter is on a long-ignored nonviolent stream within the Gospels evident in the words and actions of the historical Jesus. The ten core passages discussed demonstrate that Jesus didn't believe Roman imperialism was God's punishment for sin. He sees promises of liberation or vindication through God's violence as dangerous myths, "fantasy freedoms" that keep the people in bondage and feed a destructive spiral of violence. Jesus embraces the nonviolent power of God. He rejects end-of-the-world scenarios (apocalyptic expectations) and to our surprise also seems to reject the idea that God would send a messiah to save Israel or us. Jesus says God's power is invitational rather than coercive. He models and calls forth creative nonviolence. He describes God's realm as modest and already present, not as grandiose and a future event. Jesus sees God as infinitely giving and invites us to embrace abundant life, to love enemies, to be mindful of daily miracles, and to be compassionate.

PASSAGE 1: LOVE ENEMIES

You have heard that it was said, "You shall love your neighbor and hate your enemy." But I say to you, Love your enemies and pray for those who persecute you, so that you may be children of your Father in heaven ... [who] makes the sun rise on the evil and on the good, and sends rain on the righteous and the unrighteous. (Matt 5:43–45)

These are among the most radical and most unexpected verses in the Bible. Love of neighbor was well attested within the Hebrew scriptures

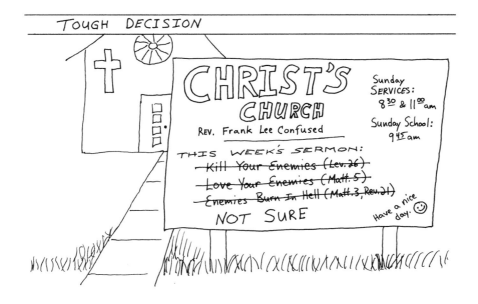

and a common expectation of faithful Jews, but love of enemies was not. Jesus' counsel would have offended many of his contemporaries beyond the Essenes who embraced hatred of enemies as part of their foundational creed. Hatred of enemies is implied on page after page of the Hebrew scriptures. The national theology and mythology centered on an interpretation of the Exodus in which God is God because of superior violence directed against the enemies of the chosen people. Exile is explained as God's punishing violence against the chosen people now become enemies of God through sin. And the overwhelming definition of salvation is the crushing defeat of enemies either within or at the end of history.

Both the weather and the defeat of enemies were understood as conditional blessings. "If you follow my statutes and keep my commandments . . . I will give you your rains in their season. . . . You shall give chase to your enemies, and they shall fall before you by the sword" (Lev 26:3, 4, 7). Jesus rejects these views. John Dominic Crossan comments on Jesus' radical call to love enemies, "I can only interpret it as commanding absolute nonviolence."[1]

PASSAGE 2: SAVED BY ENEMIES

[The hated Samaritan] went to him and bandaged his wounds, having poured oil and wine on them. Then he put him on his own animal, brought him to an inn, and took care of him. (Luke 10:34)

Jesus goes beyond a call to love enemies and says pointedly in a parable about a "compassionate Samaritan" (Luke 10:29–37) that we are saved by our enemies. Samaritans were hated by other Jews because they had intermarried during a time of foreign occupation. This was no small matter in a society preoccupied with holiness. Ezra explained exile as God's punishment because "the holy seed has mixed itself with the peoples of the lands" (Ezra 9:2). He forced the people to separate themselves from "the peoples of the lands and from the foreign wives" (Ezra 10:11) so that the "fierce wrath of our God on this account is averted from us" (Ezra 10:14b).

In Jesus' parable a Jew is beaten and left by the roadside. He is passed by and left for dead by a priest and a Levite but is helped by a hated Samaritan. Jesus lampoons salvation as defeat of enemies by telling a story in which the compassion of a hated enemy saves a beaten Jew. I have written elsewhere about what it might mean for us to be saved by our enemies in the post–September 11, 2001, world.[2] Walter Wink offers a flavor of its potential meaning:

> [This is] the gift our enemy may be able to bring us: *to see aspects of ourselves that we cannot discover any other way than through our enemies.* Our friends seldom tell us these things; they are our friends precisely because they are able to overlook or ignore this part of us. The enemy is thus not merely a hurdle to be leaped on the way to God. The enemy *can be* the way to God. We cannot come to terms with our shadow except through our enemies, for we have almost no other access to those unacceptable parts of ourselves that need redeeming except through the mirror that our enemies hold up to us. This then is another, more intimate reason for loving our enemies.... We may not be whole people without them.[3]

PASSAGE 3: THE SPIRAL OF VIOLENCE

Then he began to speak to them in parables. "A man planted a vineyard, put a fence around it, dug a pit for the wine press, and built a watchtower; then he leased it to tenants and went to another country. When the season came, he sent a slave to the tenants to collect from them his share of the produce of the vineyard. But they seized him, and beat him, and sent him away empty-handed. And again he sent another slave to them; this one they beat over the head and insulted. Then he sent another, and that one they killed. And so it was with many others; some they beat, and others they killed. He had still one other, a beloved son. Finally he sent him to them, saying, 'They will respect my son.' But those tenants said to one another, 'This is the heir; come, let us kill him, and the inheritance will be ours.' So they seized him, killed him, and threw him out of the vineyard. What then will the owner of the vineyard do? He will come and destroy the tenants and give the vineyard to others." (Mark 12:1–9)

A common assumption in Jesus' time and our own is that of redemptive violence, the widespread belief that superior violence saves. In Exodus theology God proves to be God through superior violence. Hope rooted in "liberating violence" is at the heart of prophetic promises of historical reversals and is central to the understanding of salvation as defeat of enemies. Although violent rebellions near the time of Jesus' birth were crushed by Rome, violent protest was both reality and temptation as indicated by widespread social banditry, Sicarii dagger attacks, and Zealot rebellion.

Oppressive systems require resistance. But how are we to resist? Jesus critiques and encourages discussion of violent resistance to oppression in a parable whose social setting mirrors that of many of his contemporaries in rural Galilee. Peasants had always paid an outrageous percentage of their crops for taxes and tithes, but now they were losing their land due to debt. The wealthy absentee owners that replaced the peasant owners often planted vineyards to raise grapes that could be turned into wine, an exportable commodity. Jesus tells a parable about a vineyard owner in order to expose deadly dynamics in the oppressive system, including the futility of violent rebellion.

The characters and dynamics of the parable are familiar. A man plants a vineyard, builds a watchtower, leases it to tenants, and leaves. At harvest time he sends a slave to collect his share. The workers seize the slave, beat him, and send him away empty-handed. The vineyard owner sends another slave who is beaten and insulted and then another whom the tenants kill. Many others are sent only to be beaten or killed. Finally, the vineyard owner sends his son to collect his share of the harvest. The workers "seized him, killed him and threw him out of the vineyard." Jesus then asks and answers an ominous question: "What then will the owner of the vineyard do? He will come and destroy the tenants and give the vineyard to others."

This parable is often interpreted as a story about "wicked tenants" and its meaning has been thoroughly theologized by Mark, who turns an oppressive absentee owner into a God-figure. Mark and interpreters that follow his lead are not interested in what Jesus said and meant in the context of the oppressive system. They seek rather to show why Jesus was rejected and to demonstrate that his rejection fulfilled God's promises as recorded in the Hebrew scriptures. Mark places a scriptural quotation on Jesus' lips: "The stone that the builders rejected has become the cornerstone; this was the Lord's doing, and it is amazing in our eyes" (vv. 10–11). William Herzog describes the parable's meaning for Mark and most interpreters:

> The man who planted the vineyard is Yahweh, and the vineyard itself refers to Israel whether as a historical manifestation of God's people or as God's kingdom.... The tenants are the leaders of Israel, specifically, the Jerusalem authorities; the servants are the prophets sent by God; and the "beloved son"... is Jesus himself, the culminating messenger and servant.... "The others" refers to the emerging church as the new vineyard of God whose leaders will become the new tenants of the vineyard.[4]

Herzog then invites us to look at parables differently. He says that "parables were not earthly stories with heavenly meanings but earthy stories with heavy meanings" that shed light on "the reigning systems of oppression."[5] Herzog renames this parable "Peasant Revolt and the Spiral of Violence,"[6] based on a concept from liberation theology that describes violence in relation to three spokes. The first spoke, violence no. 1, is oppression. The second spoke, violence no. 2, is rebellion. People who are oppressed (no. 1) often use violent means to resist (no. 2) and this leads to the third spoke, violence no. 3, which is repression. The spiral of violence can't be broken using violent means. Violent resistance triggers repressive violence, says Herzog, and the deadly spiral escalates and deepens.

Returning to the parable, peasants had good reasons to resent wealthy landowners who pushed them off their ancestral lands and converted them into vineyards. Displaced peasants were hired to work their former lands as tenants raising the new owner's export crop. If their survival was at stake, then rebellion may have seemed the only option. As the parable unfolds, one senses the exhilaration of the oppressed tenants and those living vicariously through its telling. The humiliated humiliate others. The shamed do the shaming. The ones often killed or considered disposable kill and dispose of the body of the owner's son. The disinherited rightful heirs to the land deny the inheritance of an illegitimate heir. There must have been a feeling of power as oppression gave way to rebellion and the vicarious experience of justified revenge.

Had the parable ended here Jesus' hearers may have joined together and gone on a rampage against any deserving oppressor. But Jesus' parable includes an ominous question and response: "What then will the owner of the vineyard do? He will come and destroy the tenants and give the vineyard to others." The parable highlights the spiral of violence, underscores the futility of violent rebellion, and leaves one groping for alternative forms of protest and resistance.[7]

PASSAGE 4: CREATIVE NONVIOLENT ACTION

You have heard that it was said, "An eye for an eye and a tooth for a tooth." But I say to you, Do not resist an evildoer. But if anyone strikes you on the right cheek, turn the other also; and if anyone wants to sue you and take your coat, give your cloak as well; and if anyone forces you

to go one mile, go also the second mile. Give to everyone who begs from
you, and do not refuse anyone who wants to borrow from you.

(Matt 5:38–42)

Jesus calls for an alternative to "two deeply instinctual responses to violence: flight or fight. Jesus," Walter Wink writes, "offers a third way:
nonviolent direct action."[8] In order to understand what Jesus advocates
we need to clarify one word and examine the three cases (turn other
cheek, give cloak, walk extra mile) he uses to model nonviolent direct
action. The Greek word *anthistémi*, translated above as "resist," is used
most often as a military term. It refers to violent struggle or resistance in
military encounters.[9] The translation would more accurately read "do not
violently resist an evildoer." The Jesus Seminar captures the essence of
this verse perfectly: "Don't react violently against the one who is evil."[10]

Jesus offers exploited people in first-century Palestine three examples of
creative nonviolent resistance to oppression. Slapping, suing, and forcing
imply that someone with power is taking advantage of others who are
vulnerable. The question in each, Wink notes, "is how the oppressed can
recover the initiative and assert their human dignity in a situation that
cannot for the time being be changed."[11] Humiliation was and is a fact
of daily life for oppressed people. Wink explains the situation and reasons
for Jesus' counsel:

> A backhand slap was the usual way of admonishing inferiors. Mas-
> ters backhanded slaves; husbands, wives; parents, children; Romans,
> Jews. *We have here a set of unequal relations, in each of which retaliation*
> *would invite retribution.* The only normal response would be cow-
> ering submission.... There are among his hearers people who were
> subjected to these very indignities, forced to stifle outrage at their
> dehumanizing treatment by the hierarchical system of class, race,
> gender, age, and status, and as a result of imperial occupation. Why
> then does he counsel these already humiliated people to turn the
> other cheek? Because this action robs the oppressor of the power to
> humiliate.... The person who turns the other cheek is saying, in ef-
> fect, "Try again. Your first blow failed to achieve its intended effect.

I deny you the power to humiliate me. I am a human being just like you. Your status does not alter that fact. You cannot demean me."[12]

This unexpected behavior in a world of honor and shame, Wink notes, "would create enormous difficulties for the striker." He could escalate the conflict by turning it into a fist-fight but this would make "the other his equal. . . . He has been given notice that this underling is in fact a human being."[13]

Similar dynamics are at play in the other nonviolent actions encouraged by Jesus. If they threaten to sue you and take your outer garment (they have probably already stolen your land), then give them your underwear. Stand naked before the court, shame the system, and humiliate all who look upon you. If a Roman soldier forces you to carry his pack the legally prescribed one mile (forcing someone to go further is against the law) then keep going and throw your oppressor off balance. Going a second mile could get *him* into trouble. This may not constitute a dramatic victory, but it is something, and as Wink notes, it "is in the context of Roman military occupation that Jesus speaks" and with full awareness "of the futility of armed insurrection against Roman imperial might."[14]

These concrete examples of creative nonviolence offer compelling evidence that Jesus rejected messianic and apocalyptic fantasies that linked the defeat, destruction, or overturning of domination systems to future violent acts of God. Wink summarizes the significance of these nonviolent actions:

> To those whose lifelong pattern has been to cringe before their masters, Jesus offers a way to liberate themselves from servile actions and a servile mentality. And he asserts that they can do this *before* there is a revolution. There is no need to wait until Rome has been defeated, or peasants are landed and slaves freed. They can begin to behave with dignity and recovered humanity *now*, even under the unchanged conditions of the old order. Jesus' sense of divine immediacy has social implications. The reign of God is already breaking into the world, and it comes, not as an imposition from on high, but as the leaven slowly causing the dough to rise.[15]

PASSAGE 5: SUBVERSIVE WEEDS

*He also said, "With what can we compare the kingdom of God, or what
parable will we use for it? It is like a mustard seed, which, when sown
upon the ground, is the smallest of all the seeds on earth; yet when it is
sown it grows up and becomes the greatest of all shrubs, and puts forth
large branches, so that the birds of the air can make nests in its shade."*

(Mark 4:30–32)

The "kingdom of God" is like the tiniest of seeds. This shocking metaphor
clashes sharply with conventional wisdom that said the arrival of God's
realm would be dramatic, even cataclysmic. Isaiah promised that God was
"about to create new heavens and a new earth" (Isa 65:17). "For the Lord
will come in fire, and his chariots like the whirlwind, to pay back his anger
in fury" (66:15). All the wealth of the nations would flow to Israel "like an
overflowing stream" (66:12), and all the nations and all the kings would
see Israel's vindication and glory (62:2).

The Gospel writers didn't appreciate Jesus' humor or his rejection of
messianic and apocalyptic pretensions. They, like most of Jesus' contemporaries, found the tiny mustard seed an inadequate metaphor for the
glorious "kingdom," and so they sought to rescue the image by revising it.
The Jesus Seminar's commentary is helpful:

> The mustard seed is proverbial for its smallness. The mustard plant
> is actually an annual shrub or weed, yet in Matthew and Luke it
> becomes a tree, while in Mark it becomes the biggest of all garden
> plants. Only in Thomas does it remain simply "a large plant." The
> mustard seed is an unlikely figure of speech for God's domain in
> Jesus' original parable. His listeners would probably have expected
> God's domain to be compared to something great, not something
> small and insignificant. As the tradition was passed on it fell under
> the influence of two figures: that of the mighty cedar of Lebanon
> as a metaphor for a towering empire (Ezek 17:22–23); and that of
> the apocalyptic tree of Daniel 4:12, 20–22. In Daniel, the crown of
> the tree reaches to heaven and its branches cover the earth; under
> it dwell the beasts of the field and in its branches nest the birds

of the sky. These well-known figures undoubtedly influenced the transmission and reshaping of the original parable. In his use of this metaphor, Jesus is understating the image for comic effect: the mighty cedar is now an ordinary garden weed. This is parody. For Jesus, God's domain was a modest affair, not a new world empire. It was pervasive but unrecognized, rather than noisy and arresting.[16]

Mustard seed as metaphor flew in the face of theological, historical, and mythological expectations. Its use in direct opposition to the tree imagery in Daniel is another indication that Jesus broke with apocalyptic expectations. The book of Revelation's embellishment of Daniel's tree image should alert us that Daniel and Revelation are likely to have much in common but are far removed from Jesus' expectations of God and history. As Crossan has written:

Apocalyptic eschatology means that we (a small group, whoever we are) believe that God is going to slaughter everyone else except us. I want you to hear very clearly that apocalyptic eschatology is not just an innocent statement that the end of the world is coming soon and that if the statement's wrong, well, that's all right. Apocalyptic eschatology can corrupt the human imagination profoundly in that it imagines a God whose solution to the problems of the world is slaughter. I call it "divine ethnic cleansing." It's much better than human ethnic cleansing because it really does the job. . . . And I don't think it was the solution to the Roman Empire that Jesus had in mind.[17]

Many Jews who were socialized into the violence-of-God traditions imbedded in the three major story lines discussed in chapter 1 couldn't accept the mustard seed as metaphor for the realm of God. God's promise to Abraham was that Israel would be a great nation with inhabitants more numerous than the stars. God, according to national Exodus theology, was God because of superior violence used to defeat Israel's enemies. God the holy warrior fought alongside the chosen people when they took control of the Promised Land through genocide. God's faithful servant David conquered other nations and everlasting kingship was promised to his family line. In the context of Exile, God used empires to crush the disobedient people but Almighty God promised salvation and would one day turn God's power against arrogant empires.

In the rhythm of biblical history, bad times were nearly always followed by grandiose promises of good times. There were deep longings and expectations for a "new heaven and a new earth," a renewed "kingdom," a David-like messiah to save the people, or a harsh apocalyptic judge to impose justice, and crush evil. God, Isaiah said repeatedly, would defeat all the nations and send their wealth to Israel as foreign kings proceeded as captives into God's holy city. John the Baptist promised that evildoers were about to burn in the unquenchable fire of God's wrath. The Essenes prepared for the final battle between the forces of light and the forces of darkness.

Jesus' use of mustard seed as metaphor countered these inflated expectations and illusionary hopes. We often miss another radical aspect of this metaphor described by Crossan:

The mustard plant is dangerous even when domesticated in the garden, and is deadly when growing wild in the grain fields. . . . The point, in other words, is not just that the mustard plant starts as a proverbially small seed and grows into a shrub.... It is that it tends to take over where it is not wanted.... And that, said Jesus, was what the Kingdom was like. Like a pungent shrub with dangerous take-over properties.[18]

Most of us, like many of Jesus' contemporaries, when faced with evil and the power and resiliency of oppressive systems, bring out our giant-sized imaginations. Our hope hanging by a thread, we cling to promises of God's redemptive or apocalyptic violence. We wait for God to hand over some new weapon in the divine arsenal, only to be given a packet containing a single seed. When we complain that we do not have time for the seed to grow into a mighty cedar, Jesus tells us that our packet contains a mustard seed.

Most of us throw the seed away. We cling to illusionary messianic promises and apocalyptic fantasies that have failed to materialize over thousands of years rather than accept the seed, plant it, nurture it, and see how it grows. We continue to idealize scriptural passages in our telling and retelling of biblical stories about God's redemptive, punishing violence. God's violence is placed in service to justice and the struggle against unrepentant evil as God's pathology is shielded beneath a canopy of liberation themes. We repeat these tales even though they leave the spiral of violence intact and bring us to the brink of destruction. We may be dissatisfied with the old story lines, but under our breath we can be heard to mutter, "A mustard seed? What gives?"

Jesus invites us to work for justice, reject violence, and embrace a call to be subversive weeds. To accept this vocation, Jesus suggests, means to stop embracing violence ourselves and stop projecting violence onto God. God, according to Jesus, will never violently impose justice, not within history and not as part of an end-time judgment. Why? Because God is nonviolent. We must stop waiting for God to do what Jesus says God is incapable of doing: impose justice through violence. The alternative to violence is to embrace nonviolence, sow mustard seeds, live as communities of subversive weeds, and imitate the nonviolent compassion of God. This is where abundant life is to be found.

PASSAGE 6: ABUNDANCE, NOT SCARCITY

That's why I tell you: Don't fret about your life — what you're going to eat and drink — or about your body — what you're going to wear. There is more to living than food and clothing, isn't there? Take a look at the birds of the sky: they don't plant or harvest, or gather into barns. Yet your heavenly Father feeds them. You're worth more than they, aren't you? Can any of you add one hour to life by fretting about it? Why worry about clothes? Notice how the wild lilies grow: they don't slave and they never spin. Yet let me tell you, even Solomon at the height of his glory was never decked out like one of them. If God dresses up the grass in the field, which is here today and tomorrow is thrown into an oven, won't God care for you even more, you who don't take anything for granted.

(Matt 6:25–30)[19]

Jesus looked at the world with a no-holds-barred honesty and saw abundance, not scarcity. The source of abundance was God, the Spirit imbedded in all life, surrounding us at all times and in all places inviting us to new life. Jesus walked hand-in-hand with the marginalized, and he challenged the system responsible for their poverty, but as he did so, he saw the possibility of abundant life rooted in the abundance of God. It is the reality of God's abundance that makes injustice so offensive. Injustice is a betrayal of God's character and of God's intentions for humanity and creation. Jesus experienced the reality of God as abundant love, not a limited good available to some but not to others.

Many biblical stories, including core themes in the three story lines discussed earlier, assume scarcity of goods and God. The presumption of scarcity is central to biblical stories of brotherly conflicts in which violence is an underlying theme (Cain/Abel, Jacob/Esau, Joseph/Joseph's brothers). In those stories, Regina Schwartz writes, "there is not enough divine favor, not enough blessing. . . . One can prosper only at the other's expense."[20] She notes that "the One God is not imagined as infinitely giving, but as strangely withholding. Everyone does not receive divine blessings. Some are cursed — with dearth and with death — as though there were a cosmic shortage of prosperity."[21]

Jesus sees and experiences a God infinitely giving. Against the limited blessing of the covenant in which rain is a conditional blessing linked to obedience (Lev 26:4), Jesus says that God makes the sun rise on the evil and the good and sends rain on the righteous and the unrighteous (Matt 5:45). This is simply the way God is. God's abundance is at the heart of our invitation to love enemies, to share goods, and to engage in creative active nonviolence when we resist oppression or seek justice (Matt 5:38–45).

Jesus, mindful of the heart of God, sees, experiences, and trusts the abundance of God. We are to pray for food sufficient for the day (Matt 6:11) and imitate the generosity of God. "Give to everyone who begs from you" (Matt 5:42). The feeding of the five thousand is a story in which scarcity and hoarding give way to sharing and unexpected abundance (Mark 6:30–44). Jesus laments the conduct of a wealthy landowner who pulls down his barns and builds larger ones to store grain that belongs this day to God (Luke 12:13–21), and he tells a parable of a great dinner to which all are invited "and there is still room" (Luke 14:15–24).

God's abundance and our embrace of abundant life should never be equated with riches or affluence (Mark 10:17–25) but with mindfulness and sufficiency. God, who provides for the birds and gives us the miraculous beauty of the lilies, wants us to notice and provides abundance sufficient for all. "That's why I tell you: Don't fret about your life — what you're going to eat and drink — or about your body — what you're going to wear. There is more to living than food and clothing, isn't there?" The Buddhist peacemaker Thich Nhat Hanh describes mindfulness and captures the essence of Jesus' vision when he writes: "When we are mindful, touching deeply the present moment, we can see and listen deeply, and the fruits are always understanding, acceptance, love, and the desire to relieve suffering and bring joy."[22]

Faithfully embracing the abundance of God would do much to end the spiral of violence rooted in scarcity, competition, and longed for reversals associated with the redemptive violence. There is, according to Jesus, plenty of blessing, goods, and compassion for everyone if we are mindful of God's abundance and if we accept God's invitation to abundant life.

PASSAGE 7: GRACE UNLIMITED

*I will get up and go to my father, and I will say to him, "Father, I have
sinned against heaven and before you; I am no longer worthy to be called
your son; treat me like one of your hired hands." So he set off and went
to his father. But while he was still far off, his father saw him and was
filled with compassion; he ran and put his arms around him and kissed
him.* (Luke 15:18–20)

Jesus' parable of the prodigal son (Luke 15:11–32) represents a dramatic
reversal of expectations concerning the punishing character of God. A
father agrees to his younger son's request for his inheritance, which he
quickly squanders in irresponsible living. After falling into destitution,
including eating the food of swine, the younger son decides to return
home and beg his father for mercy so that he might live as a hired hand.
As soon as his father sees him, however, and before the younger son can
ask for mercy, the father "was filled with compassion; he ran and put his
arms around him and kissed him" (v. 20).

Without acknowledging his son's apology, the father sends word that
the fatted calf is to be slaughtered so that the son's return can be cele-
brated. The older son then enters the story. He is furious because from his
perspective the wayward son is being treated far better than he deserves
and better than the faithful older son himself. The older son's attitudes
and behavior reflect earlier brother conflict stories as noted above. The
older son sees himself in competition with his brother for inheritance, acceptance, and blessing. His view of the world is clearly foreign to the ways
of the father. The younger son receives the undeserved compassion of the
father simply because that is the way the father is and the way the father
sees the world.

In this parable Jesus shatters expectations of a punishing Deity. He
portrays God as the source of unlimited and undeserved compassion and
the world as a place of plenty. Forgiveness is, according to Jesus, the
character of God. Forgiveness is available to us without our asking. Jesus
experiences God as infinitely giving and forgiving and invites us to imitate
the unlimited forgiveness of God (Matt 18:22).

PASSAGE 8: INVITATIONAL JUDGMENT, INVITATIONAL POWER, NONVIOLENT GOD

Then Jesus said to him, "Someone gave a great dinner and invited many. At the time for the dinner he sent his slave to say to those who had been invited, 'Come; for everything is ready now.' But they all alike began to make excuses. The first said to him, 'I have bought a piece of land, and I must go out and see it; please accept my regrets.' Another said, 'I have bought five yoke of oxen, and I am going to try them out; please accept my regrets.' Another said, 'I have just been married, and therefore I cannot come.' So the slave returned and reported this to his master. Then the owner of the house became angry and said to his slave, 'Go out at once into the streets and lanes of the town and bring in the poor, the crippled, the blind, and the lame.' And the slave said, 'Sir, what you ordered has been done, and there is still room.' Then the master said to the slave, 'Go out into the roads and the lanes, and compel people to come in, so that my house may be filled. For I tell you, none of those who were invited will taste my dinner.'" (Luke 14:16–24)

This story reflects a notion of God's judgment and God's power remarkably different from those described in Exile theology and in much of Matthew's Gospel. God, according to the prophets, orchestrates the destruction of Israel and reduces the people to cannibalism as punishment for sin. Matthew's Jesus threatens people with eternal fires and weeping and gnashing of teeth. The book of Revelation describes those who will "drink the wine of God's wrath, poured unmixed into the cup of his anger" so as to be "tormented with fire and sulfur in the presence of the holy angels and in the presence of the Lamb." In sharp contrast, this Lukan passage moves markedly in the direction of a noncoercive vision of God's power. Instead of threats and a scarcity of God's blessing, we have an open invitation to dinner that includes everybody. Not everyone accepts the invitation but exclusion from dinner is the choice of those who are preoccupied with other things.

God invites rich people to the dinner. Most are too busy to come. God then invites those specifically excluded from the Qumran community because they would be inadequate fighters in the coming final confrontation with the forces of darkness: "the poor, the crippled, the blind, and the

THE WORD OF THE LORD

"See, the day of the Lord comes, cruel, with wrath and fierce anger, to make the earth a desolation, and to destroy sinners from it... So four angels were released to kill a third of human kind... And these will go away into eternal punishment... and there will be weeping and gnashing of teeth." This is the word of the Lord.

THANKS BE TO GOD!

lame." God is so determined that people come to dinner that servants are instructed to "compel people to come in." This is a far cry from compelling people to live in outer darkness or excluding them from the community because of sin, nonpayment of tithes, lack of holiness, or other matters of ritual purity.

The Jesus Seminar sees verse 24 of Luke as "a Lukan addition. Luke," it notes, "excludes the Pharisees, who reject the invitation to the (messianic) banquet."[23] Even if we include this verse as part of Jesus' original story, however, the only sanction is that some invited guests "will not taste" the dinner because they reject the invitation. They miss abundant life because they are preoccupied with other things of their own choosing. In other words, Jesus invites all to live and experience abundant life here and now in the presence of God's invitational Spirit, but our choices determine whether or not abundant life is experienced.

It would be hard to imagine more striking differences concerning the nature of God's judgment between the portrayal here and that noted earlier in Matthew.[24] Judgment, according to this parable, is not something a powerful, punishing God does to individuals or nations who make mistakes. It is self-exclusion. If we miss the beckoning of the Spirit and make bad choices, then we miss abundant life. I call this "invitational judgment" because abundant life and whether others have a decent life depends on acceptance or rejection of an invitation that is open to all and available always. The important thing about invitational judgment, and this is hard for many of us to accept, is that God's power can't force us to live justly nor punish us for being unjust. Our acceptance or refusal of the invitation to abundant life has consequences for ourselves and others, but God's invitational power excludes the punishing sanctions of a violent Deity. The result of my bad choices is that I miss out on abundant life and hurt others. The result of collective refusal of the Spirit's invitation can be catastrophic, not because of God's punishing violence, but because our choices lead to war and not peace, inequality and not shared gifts, environmental stress and not caretaking of the earth.

The invitational power of God includes our invitation to take Jesus' radical nonviolence seriously and to imitate the nonviolent power of God. As Crossan writes, the radical ethic of Jesus reflects "a style of life for now rather than a hope for the future."[25] It is "nonviolent resistance to structural violence. It is absolute faith in a nonviolent God and the attempt to live and act in union with such a God."[26]

PASSAGE 9: NO MESSIAH TO SAVE US

When he began the reckoning, one who owed him ten thousand talents was brought to him. . . . And out of pity for him, the lord of that slave released him and forgave him the debt. But that same slave, as he went out, came upon one of his fellow slaves who owed him a hundred denarii; and seizing him by the throat, he said, "Pay what you owe." (Matt 18:24, 27–28)

Jews expected, and occasionally announced the arrival of, a messiah in Israel to reestablish Israel's privileged and powerful place among the nations,

purge the defiled land of imperialism, and replace the Temple's collaborative priestly rulers. Jesus dismissed these expectations. The temptation
narrative (Matt 4:1–11; Luke 4:1–12) indicates that Jesus rejected messianic expectations and their implicit and explicit understandings of God
and history. There would be no one sent by God to miraculously do away
with hunger, inspire proper belief and practices by performing miracles at
the Temple, or rule over Israel and the nations.

Jesus' rejection of the popular idea that a messiah would free Israel is
one likely reading of the parable of the unmerciful servant (Matt 18:23–
35). The parable depicts a king who forgives the enormous debt of one
of his "slaves" who can't pay and begs for forgiveness. This slave leaves
the king and encounters someone who owes him a substantial but far
smaller debt than the one the king just canceled to his benefit. Rather
than reciprocate the king's generosity he treats the debtor harshly. He,
in stark contrast to the king, refuses the debtor's plea for mercy and has
the debtor thrown into prison. When the king hears of it he is outraged
and turns the slave "over to be tortured until he would pay his entire
debt" (v. 34).

William Herzog sees the "slave" as a bureaucratic retainer and he under-
stands the parable as Jesus' direct challenge to false messianic expectations
and promises. Jesus understood that although oppressed people long for,
need, and deserve justice, hope rooted in a messiah was false hope. The
present parable addresses this issue because the Jewish messiah was expected to cancel debts as part of the overthrow of the oppressive system.
"The opening scene of the parable," Herzog writes, "depicts a messianic
moment, not in spiritualized terms but in an earthy economic image of a
king canceling debt. . . . If the largest amount of debt imaginable has been
canceled, then the messianic king has arrived and the messianic age has
begun."[27] In this reading, the king is a messianic figure who announces
forgiveness of debt only to have the messianic moment unravel. His long
hoped for action turns sour because oppression is rooted in an entrenched,
exploitative bureaucracy. Herzog writes:

> But the [messianic] moment is short-lived. No sooner has the new
> age of debt forgiveness been inaugurated than it is canceled by the

cutthroat tactics of a typical powerful bureaucrat.... Backed into a corner, the king reverts with a vengeance to business as usual, delivering the courtier to the torturers.... Whether expressed in the traditions of popular kingship or in other forms of messianic hope, the reliance on a future king to rescue the people from debt and bondage harbored a fatal, unnoticed contradiction. Kingship was an institution embedded in a bureaucratic system.[28]

Just as tenants got a temporary rush from the vicarious experience of justified revenge only to be brought back to reality by Jesus' ominous question ("What then will the owner of the vineyard do?"), so it is with the hearers of this parable. Jubilation over the arrival of the messianic moment dies fast. Kingship in Israel rarely if ever lived up to the hopes of the Psalmist for justice and righteousness (Ps 72:1–4). In the context of the spiral of violence, Jesus rejected messianic promises and expectations that a popular king or messiah would emerge to solve pressing problems rooted in a well-entrenched, highly bureaucratized system involving kings and priests, retainers, scribes, and other mid-level functionaries. The system had to be exposed but so too did false messianic promises and pretensions that masked but could never overcome despair. False messianic promises and expectations, Jesus suggested, stifle authentic hope. It is a great and tragic irony that with the aid of Gospel distortions Christianity turned Jesus into a largely otherworldly messiah after Jesus' own life, faith, and experience of God led him to reject messianic expectations.

PASSAGE 10: APOCALYPSE NEVER, GOD'S PRESENT REALM

Once Jesus was asked by the Pharisees when the kingdom of God was coming, and he answered, "The kingdom of God is not coming with things that can be observed; nor will they say, 'Look, here it is!' or 'There it is!' For, in fact, the kingdom of God is among you." (Luke 17:20–21)

Historical catastrophes in first-century Palestine created conditions ripe for a groundswell of apocalyptic expectations and interpretations of events. This explains why the apocalyptic stream in the New Testament nearly

overwhelms other aspects of the Jesus story. Paul understood Jesus' resurrection as an apocalyptic event marking the beginning of the end time.
He expected the general resurrection and culmination of history within
his lifetime. The Gospel writers found the apocalyptic worldview helpful
for three reasons. It served as a lens to make sense of Jesus' crucifixion.
It provided an explanation for why God allowed the Jewish Temple and
Jerusalem to be destroyed during the Roman-Jewish war of 66–70. And
it served as ideological window dressing for growing Christian hatred and
desired revenge against Jews who rejected Jewish Christian claims that
Jesus fulfilled God's promises as laid out in the Hebrew scriptures.

The crucifixion of Jesus sent literate Jewish followers back to their sacred traditions in an effort to find clues as to why he had been killed.
It was impossible to convince many Jews that Jesus or anyone else who
had been brutally crucified had fulfilled a tradition rooted in messianic
promises of historical triumph. The Gospel writers, therefore, interpreted
the meaning of Jesus' life and death largely in relation to apocalyptic expectations framed in the book of Daniel. Vindication, Daniel said, would
come at the end time, not within history. The crucifixion of Jesus was
understood by the Gospel writers as an instrument in God's divine plan
and his resurrection initiated the general resurrection that was linked to
apocalyptic end time promises. Jesus the cosmic judge would return soon
as the apocalypse personified, the Son of Man.

The apocalyptic interpretation of Jesus had the additional advantage of
responding to the desire for revenge that arose from the intense pain of
rejection felt by Jewish Christians after the vast majority of Jews rebuffed
their claims. These Jews did not fare well in Gospel accounts. They were
blamed for the murder of Jesus and their rejection of Jesus was used to
explain Rome's destruction of Jerusalem and the Temple. It was only a
small step to make God's punishment permanent. Those who rejected
Jesus would face the same harsh fate as all enemies of God: they would fry.
The transformation or, better said, *deformation* of Jesus, is astounding. The
nonviolent Jewish Jesus who taught love of enemies, revealed a nonviolent
God, and inspired alternatives to the domination system within history,
became God's murderous apocalyptic accomplice who would return soon
to violently judge and crush enemies and all evildoers at the end of history.

APOCALYPTIC HOPE

None of the images of God and actions of Jesus described above, including love of enemies, salvation through enemies, breaking the spiral of violence, creative nonviolent action, the call to be subversive weeds, abundance, unlimited grace, invitational power, and a nonviolent God can be reconciled with the apocalyptic worldview. The parables of Jesus offer further evidence of his break with apocalyptic images of God and expectations of history. Many parables set out to help peasants understand and change their reality by exposing and positing alternatives to the oppressive system. It is hard to reconcile Jesus' parables with expectations that God is about to decisively intervene to either end history or impose justice. Jesus rejected both messianic pretensions and apocalyptic promises that divide the world neatly between good and evil and that look for easy solutions that never happen. "Had Jesus' parables indulged in apocalyptic speculation or threatened the end of the world," Herzog writes, "he would have been watched but left alone."[29] And as Robert Funk writes, of "the twenty-odd parables that are probably authentically from Jesus, the strange thing is that not one says anything about the end of the world or the apocalyptic trauma that is supposed to accompany that event."[30]

Jesus exposed injustices in the oppressive system but he also saw and experienced the abundance of God. He rejected apocalyptic and messianic promises that abundant life would come sometime in the future as a result of God's redemptive violence. We experience abundant life if and when we orient our lives to the Spirit of God. The Spirit invites us here and now and always to imitate and embody the compassion of God in our daily lives and in our social systems. It is in this context that Jesus' radical antiapocalyptic saying concerning the "kingdom" of God should be understood (Luke 17:20–21): It is not coming but already among us. Jesus doesn't root hope in promises that a violent God will act to replace or destroy oppressive systems in the near or distant future. He plants his life, his hope, and his nonviolence in the nonviolent character of God present in the world now. God's Spirit surrounds us every minute of every day and invites us here, now, everywhere, and always to abundant life in the alternative realm of God.

DISCUSSION

Our Focus: To notice and discuss the nonviolent streams of Jesus' message.

Discuss one or more of the questions in each of the four categories.

Objective Questions

1. What are some pictures of Jesus (and his teaching) that emerge from these ten passages?

2. What are the images of God that are presented in these passages?

3. What is one way (according to the author) that Jesus turns tradition, expectations, and scripture on their head?

4. What images of the "realm of God" stand out for you?

5. What is one way that Jesus appears to be challenging violence?

Reflective Questions

6. Where, if at all, did you get thrown for a loop in reading through this?

7. Where, if at all, did you have a great feeling of "Yes!"?

8. What surprised you in this chapter? What challenged you?

9. Did any of the passages give you a particularly strong feeling? What feeling?

Interpretive Questions

10. Which of the ten passages is your favorite? Why?

11. Where did you disagree with Jesus? With the New Testament authors?

12. Are you comfortable with Jesus' modest claims about the "realm of God"?

13. Do you think there are ways we are "saved by our enemies"?

14. "Consider the lilies of the field...." What is the essence of mindfulness?

15. Was nonviolence realistic in Jesus' time? In our own time?

16. Could the Gospel writers be wrong about Jesus?

17. These ten passages are only a small portion of the four Gospels. Is it accurate to lift them out and say, "This is the thrust of the authentic Jesus"? What issues are raised in doing so?

Decisional Questions

18. What would it mean for our congregation to take "love of enemies" seriously?

19. Based on this chapter what will change for you about how you view Jesus' message? What issues should our congregation be wrestling with? What question would you like this group to consider?

ACTIVITY

Creative Writing

Either now or at a future session, divide into small groups and allow ten to fifteen minutes for one of the following. Then come together and share results. Remind folks that the goal is not perfection but "rough draft" quality.

Option 1. Come up with a slogan for a banner to hang in the sanctuary using the message you feel most strongly about from this chapter.

Option 2. Pick a contemporary issue such as poverty, inequality, or globalization and write a parable "in the spirit of Jesus."

Option 3. Write two new verses for the tune of "Amazing Grace," one verse that poses a question and one that gives an answer in the spirit of Jesus. Sing with the group.

Short Skit

Pick one of the ten passages and develop a short skit that portrays something important for you about Jesus' message.

The Debate Team

Divide into two groups for an agree/disagree debate on the topic, "The world is such a mess today that nonviolence as an approach to life and problems is not realistic." Assign one group to agree and another to disagree. Allow ten minutes for each group to discuss and prepare separately and then stage the debate. Give each side two minutes to present. Then give each side two minutes for rebuttal. Close by sharing, "How did this process feel?"

NOTES

1. John Dominic Crossan, *The Birth of Christianity: Discovering What Happened in the Years Immediately after the Execution of Jesus* (San Francisco: HarperSanFrancisco, 1998), 391.

2. See Jack Nelson-Pallmeyer, *Is Religion Killing Us? Violence in the Bible and the Quran* (Harrisburg, Pa.: Trinity Press International, 2003), chapter 8.

3. Walter Wink, *Engaging the Powers: Discernment and Resistance in a World of Domination* (Minneapolis: Fortress Press, 1992), 273, emphasis in original.

4. William R. Herzog II, *Parables as Subversive Speech: Jesus as Pedagogue of the Oppressed* (Louisville: Westminster/John Knox Press, 1994), 101.

5. Ibid., 3, 7.

6. Ibid., chapter 6.

7. Much of this analysis is found in Nelson-Pallmeyer, *Jesus against Christianity* (Harrisburg, Pa.: Trinity Press International, 2001), 252–59.

8. Wink, *Engaging the Powers*, 175.

9. Ibid., 185.

10. Robert W. Funk, Roy W. Hoover, and the Jesus Seminar, *The Five Gospels: The Search for the Authentic Words of Jesus* (New York: Scribner, 1993), 143. The Jesus Seminar is a group of religious scholars representing a variety of religious traditions and academic institutions. Scholars associated with the seminar have examined and inventoried all the surviving ancient texts for words attributed to Jesus and have offered their judgments as to which of these words are authentically traceable to Jesus and which reflect the views of the Gospel writers or editors rather than Jesus.

11. Wink, *Engaging the Powers*, 182.

12. Ibid., 176, emphasis in original.

13. Ibid.

14. Ibid., 181.

15. Ibid., 183, emphasis in original. See Nelson-Pallmeyer, *Jesus against Christianity*, 324–326.

16. Funk, Hoover, and the Jesus Seminar, *The Five Gospels*, 484.

17. John Dominic Crossan, "Jesus and the Kingdom: Itinerants and Householders in Earliest Christianity," in *Jesus at 2000*, ed. Marcus Borg (Boulder, Colo.: Westview Press, 1997), 51–52.

18. John Dominic Crossan, *Jesus: A Revolutionary Biography* (New York: HarperCollins, 1995), 65.

19. Funk, Hoover, and the Jesus Seminar, *The Five Gospels*, 151–52.

20. Regina M. Schwartz, *The Curse of Cain: The Violent Legacy of Monotheism* (Chicago: University of Chicago Press, 1997), 4.

21. Ibid., 3.

22. Thich Nhat Hanh, *Living Buddha, Living Christ* (New York: Riverhead Books, 1995), 14.

23. Funk, Hoover, and the Jesus Seminar, *The Five Gospels*, 352.

24. For an interesting look at Matthew's violent and rather vile version of this parable (22:1–14) see Nelson-Pallmeyer, *Jesus against Christianity*, 314–15.

25. Crossan, *Jesus*, 56.

26. Crossan, *Birth of Christianity*, 287.

27. Herzog, *Parables as Subversive Speech*, 147.

28. Ibid.

29. Ibid., 27.

30. Robert Funk, *Honest to Jesus: Jesus for a New Millennium* (San Francisco: HarperSanFrancisco, 1996), 69.

CHAPTER 4

IN THE SPIRIT OF JESUS

The nonviolent stream connected to the historical Jesus is rooted in images of God and expectations of history radically different from those that dominate much of the Bible and Christian tradition. The present chapter makes an explicit case that we need to re-ritualize Christianity in light of this stream.

NONVIOLENT STREAM IGNORED

The biblical writers shaped their images of God (and ours) in relation to explanations and expectations of history that Jesus rejected. The violent tradition discussed in chapter 1 says that God acts in history or at the end time with liberating, punishing, or vindicating violence. The nonviolent stream associated with Jesus says hope rooted in God's violence is false hope. Jesus models nonviolent resistance and celebrates the invitational, nonviolent power of God.

Central to the violent tradition is Exodus theology's emphasis on God's liberating violence. God proves to be God through superior violence, and salvation means defeat of enemies. The nonviolent stream invites us to work for justice, but Jesus rejects human or divine violence as a means to justice. He associates salvation with healing and wholeness.

At the heart of the violent tradition's Exile theology is belief that Israel's historical situation is the direct consequence of obedience or sin. The promised fruits of obedience include good rains, good harvests, defeat of enemies, and security. The promised fruits of disobedience are defeat by enemies, subjugation, exile, or destruction.[1] The nonviolent stream linked to Jesus, by way of contrast, doesn't see Roman imperialism as God's punishment. The Rome-Temple dominated system is counter to God's intentions and is the unfortunate reality in which people are called to live authentic lives, work for justice, build community, practice hospitality, engage in nonviolent resistance, and embody God's compassion. Jesus portrays God unconditionally providing rain, sunshine, and the possibility of new life.

The prophets of the violent tradition announce God's judgment, call for repentance, and promise a historical reversal of fortunes in which the now oppressed Israelites will oppress their oppressors. The nonviolent stream associated with Jesus seeks to break the spiral of violence that is evident in illusionary promises that fester at the heart of most systems of injustice and many of the following biblical stories.

Joseph utilizes food as a weapon on behalf of the Pharaoh. As a result, all Egyptians end up penniless, landless, and enslaved (Gen 47). Resentments flower. The powerful Israelites suffer when a new Pharaoh takes control. Hatreds explode and violence thrives and survives numerous reversals. The Israelites groan amid their oppression and with God's help fight back and win. In the aftermath of Pharaoh's defeat, lands are stolen, and the chosen people carry out "divinely sanctioned" genocide (Exodus).

Elijah wins a contest with the priests of Baal and then executes them (2 Kings 18:35–40). Israelites, unable to sing the Lord's song in captivity, anticipate the happy day when they will smash the heads of their captors' children against the rocks (Ps 137:9). Isaiah announces that God will come "with vengeance," "save" the people, and "spare no one" (Isa 35:4; 47:3). The kings who took Jewish leaders into exile will be humiliated and the wealth of the nations will flow to Israel (Isa 49:23).

Daniel walks away from the lion's den and immediately "those who had accused Daniel were brought and thrown into the den of lions — they, their children, and their wives. Before they reached the bottom of the den the lions overpowered them and broke their bones in pieces" (Dan 6:24).

Mary announces salvation that lifts up the poor and sends the rich away with nothing (Luke 1:52–54). Jesus, mindful of God and the destructiveness of this never-ending cycle, promotes nonviolent resistance and seeks to break the spiral of violence.

The violent tradition's Apocalyptic theology emerges after centuries of unfulfilled prophetic promises. It is utterly pessimistic about human prospects within history. God is fighting a cosmic battle between good and evil in heaven and is thus preoccupied and unable to redeem Israel. The good news is that God will soon win the cosmic battle and a new violent coming of God is imminent. God will crush evil, punish evildoers, resurrect and vindicate the faithful, and end history. The nonviolent stream connected to Jesus lampoons these wild fantasies with humor, including stories of mustard seeds, and with practical suggestions for daily life and resistance. Jesus shares food, tells parables that expose and call forth alternatives to the system, engages in creative civil disobedience, builds community, embraces hospitality, and announces that God's realm is not coming but is already present.

WHY DOES CHRISTIANITY IGNORE THE NONVIOLENT STREAM AND EMBRACE THE VIOLENT TRADITION?

The New Testament writers offer us glimpses into the oppressive social order, but they give us irreconcilable portraits of who Jesus was, what he said and did, and what his life and death meant. The writers include a nonviolent stream that is most visible in the words and actions of the historical Jesus. These words and actions break decisively with violent images of God embedded in the tradition. This stream, however, is largely ignored or undermined by the *theology* of the Gospel writers and traditional Christian theology that interprets and positions Jesus in relation to the violent traditions that he rejected. As a result, elements of the violent traditions are featured centrally and the nonviolent stream is marginalized within traditional Christian theology, worship, music, and liturgies. This can be illustrated by a brief look at the apocalyptic and sacrificial lenses that serve as interpretive keys for the New Testament writers and much of traditional Christianity.

JESUS: APOCALYPSE NEVER; GOSPEL WRITERS: APOCALYPSE NOW

Jesus rejects the apocalyptic worldview, but the New Testament writers make sense of his life and death through an apocalyptic lens. Paul didn't know Jesus, but he had a mystical experience and concluded that the resurrection of Jesus was the beginning of the end of the world. Mark, the first Gospel written, begins with Jesus being baptized by an apocalyptic prophet, and the New Testament ends with Christ returning to terminate history as an apocalyptic judge in the book of Revelation. Matthew attributes nearly identical apocalyptic words to Jesus and John the Baptist (Matt 3:7–12, 7:19, 23:33). Most important, the Gospel writers take the image of "one like a human being" from the book of Daniel (7:13–14) and transform it, and the nonviolent Jesus, into the apocalyptic "Son of Man." The "Son of Man" is portrayed often as a violent judge. In Matthew it is the "Son of Man" who will come to separate the sheep who are destined for "eternal life" from the goats who "will go away into eternal punishment" (25:31, 46). Luke leaves no doubt that for Luke Jesus is the apocalyptic "Son of Man." Luke places these words on the lips of Jesus in order to bolster apocalyptic expectations linking Jesus to God's violent power:

> But from now on the Son of Man will be seated at the right hand of the power of God." All of them asked, "Are you, then, the Son of God?" He said to them, "You say that I am." Then they said, "What further testimony do we need? We have heard it ourselves from his own lips! (Luke 22:69–71)

Consistent with the apocalyptic profile, the "Son of Man" will come unexpectedly but soon to end the world, vindicate the faithful, and crush evil. Verses from Mark's mini-apocalypse, also found in Matthew, read:

> Then they will see "the Son of Man coming in clouds" with great power and glory. Then he will send out the angels, and gather his elect from the four winds, from the ends of the earth to the ends of heaven.... Truly I tell you, this generation will not pass away until all these things have taken place. (Mark 13:26–27, 30)

Apocalyptic themes also dominate the book of Revelation. God or God's angels, often in the presence of the Lamb (Jesus), vindicate the saints by killing much of humanity and punishing evildoers: "They will also drink the wine of God's wrath, poured unmixed into the cup of his

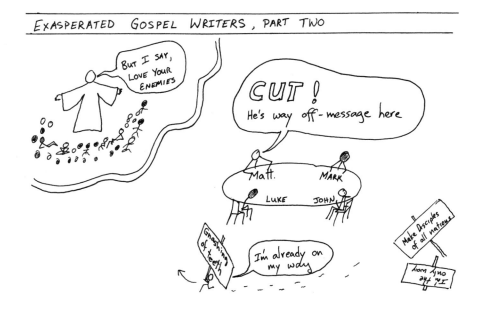

anger, and they will be tormented with fire and sulfur in the presence of the holy angels and in the presence of the Lamb. And the smoke of their torment goes up forever and ever" (Rev 14:10–11a). As Walter Wink notes, apocalyptic expectations are "filled with a craving, not for redemptive violence, but something even worse: punitive violence, to be carried out by God. . . . We are a long, long way from Jesus here."[2]

JESUS: APOCALYPSE NEVER; TRADITION: APOCALYPSE THEN AND NOW

Apocalyptic theology's violent images of God and expectations of history are far from Jesus, but they are at the heart of the Christian tradition. This contradiction can be illustrated by looking at the liturgical texts assigned for the first Sunday in Advent 2003. In the Christian calendar Advent is a season of waiting and preparation for the birth of Jesus. The assigned texts reveal that the Jesus we are waiting for is positioned in relation to violent images of God that Jesus himself rejected. We first read a promise in Jeremiah that the "days are surely coming" when someone from David's family line will "execute justice and righteousness in the land" and "save"

Judah and Jerusalem (Jer 33:14–16). The psalmist (Ps 25:1–9) then calls on "the God of my salvation" to defeat his enemies. "Do not let me be put to shame; do not let my enemies exult over me. Do not let those who wait for you be put to shame; let them be ashamed who are wantonly treacherous." This is followed by a New Testament lesson expressing hope that God will strengthen the hearts of the Thessalonians "in holiness that you may be blameless before our God and the Father at the coming of our Lord Jesus with all his saints" (1 Thess 3:13).

These passages conflict with the nonviolent stream of Jesus on all fronts. Jeremiah announces that Jerusalem and Judah will soon be saved by a Davidic messiah. The Psalmist similarly calls on God for salvation, understood as defeat of enemies, and implicit in Paul's encouragement to the Thessalonians is that Jesus is returning soon as judge and they better exemplify holiness or else. The Gospel reading for the first Sunday in Advent (Luke 21:25–36) is even more problematic. It sets the meaning of the whole Advent season in an apocalyptic light. Jesus says:

> "There will be signs in the sun, the moon, and the stars, and on the earth distress among nations confused by the roaring of the sea and the waves. People will faint from fear and foreboding of what is coming upon the world, for the powers of the heavens will be shaken. Then they will see 'the Son of Man coming in a cloud' with power and great glory. Now when these things begin to take place, stand up and raise your heads, because your redemption is drawing near."
>
> Then he told them a parable: "Look at the fig tree and all the trees; as soon as they sprout leaves you can see for yourselves and know that summer is already near. So also, when you see these things taking place, you know that the kingdom of God is near. Truly I tell you, this generation will not pass away until all things have taken place. Heaven and earth will pass away, but my words will not pass away.
>
> "Be on guard so that your hearts are not weighed down with dissipation and drunkenness and the worries of this life, and that day catch you unexpectedly, like a trap. For it will come upon all who live on the face of the whole earth. Be alert at all times, praying

that you may have the strength to escape all these things that will take place, and to stand before the Son of Man."

Immediately prior to these verses Luke's Jesus warns of imminent historical catastrophes "for these are days of vengeance, as a fulfillment of all that is written." There "will be great distress on the earth and wrath against this people."

Apocalyptic interpretations of Jesus violate the spirit of each and every passage we considered in chapter 3. Apocalypticism, however, is not the only troubling interpretive key rejected by Jesus but used by the Gospel writers and much of traditional Christianity. Sacrificial interpretations abound.

JESUS' NONVIOLENT STREAM: EMBRACE LOVING GOD; VIOLENT TRADITION: APPEASE PUNISHING GOD

Worship and sacrifices can be ways of expressing gratitude to God, but in the violent tradition they shore up portrayals of a violent Deity. For example, in the Exodus it is awe at God's superior violence that inspires belief and worship:

Israel saw the great work that the Lord did against the Egyptians. So the people feared the Lord and believed in the Lord and in his servant Moses. (Exod 14:31)

Has any god ever attempted to go and take a nation for himself from the midst of another nation, by trials, by signs and wonders, by war, by a mighty hand and an outstretched arm, and by terrifying displays of power, as the Lord your God did for you in Egypt before your very eyes? To you it was shown so that you would acknowledge that the Lord is God; there is no other besides him. (Deut 4:34–35)

And when your children ask you [about Passover], "What do you mean by this observance?" you shall say, "It is the over sacrifice to the Lord, for he passed over the houses of the Israelites in Egypt, when he struck down the Egyptians but spared our houses." And the people bowed down and worshiped. (Exod 12:26–27)

The biblical motivation for worship and sacrifice is often to appease or court the favor of a violent, punishing Deity. The desire to appease God by ridding the land of unholiness and sin lay behind the scapegoat ritual of the Day of Atonement. Known as Yom Kippur, the Day of Atonement was one of the most important of all Jewish festivals. It involved two goats. One goat was slaughtered as a "sin offering" (Lev 16:15). The other goat was called a scapegoat because it was allowed to escape into the wilderness after having the sins of the people transferred onto it. It carried the sins of the people out of the holy land:

> When he [the high priest] has finished atoning for the holy place and the tent of meeting and the altar [by sprinkling blood from the sacrificial goat], he shall present the live goat. Then Aaron shall lay both his hands on the head of the live goat, and confess over it all the iniquities of the people of Israel, and all their transgressions, all their sins, putting them on the head of the goat, and sending it away into the wilderness by means of someone designated for the task. The goat shall bear on itself all their iniquities to a barren region; and the goat shall be set free in the wilderness. (Lev 16:20–22)

The Day of Atonement was a priestly response to exile understood as God's punishment for unholiness and sin. This "annual observance [of Yom Kippur], so important in post-exilic Israel, is never mentioned in the pre-exilic literature."[3] In other words, Yom Kippur was a desperate attempt to appease a punishing God in the context of exile.

JESUS: EMBRACE LOVING GOD; CHRISTIAN TRADITION: JESUS IS THE ATONING SACRIFICE

Many distortions of Jesus are rooted in the Gospel writers' and the Christian tradition's attempts to make sense out of Jesus' death in the context of the Day of Atonement. Jesus is understood as the ultimate scapegoat or the sacrificial Lamb of God. The sins of the world are heaped onto Jesus. Jesus stands between a wrathful Deity and sinful humanity. Early in John's Gospel John the Baptist sees Jesus and declares, "Here is the Lamb of God who takes away the sin of the world" (John 1:29).

Many Christian denominations feature atonement theology centrally in their communion liturgies. For example, in one communion setting in the *Lutheran Book of Worship* the congregation sings, "Worthy is Christ, the Lamb who was slain, whose blood set us free to be people of God." In another, "Lamb of God, you take away the sin of the world." And in another still, "Lord Jesus Christ, only Son of the Father, O Lord God, Lamb of God: You take away the sin of the world; have mercy on us."[4] In the "Service of Word and Sacrament I" from *The New Century Hymnal* of the United Church of Christ the congregation sings "Lord Jesus Christ, God's only begotten one, Lord God, Lamb of God, you take away the sin of the world." A pastoral prayer gives thanks that "Christ lived among us to reveal the mystery of your Word, to suffer and die on the cross for us." The congregation later sings "Lamb of God, you take away the sin of the world."[5] This same atonement theology can be found in the worship resources of most Protestant and Catholic liturgies.

Another carryover from the violent tradition's Exodus theology is the idea that the blood sacrifice from a perfect victim is the key to avoiding God's punishing violence. According to the Passover story in which the firstborn of all Egyptians are killed while Israelites are spared, God knew which houses to avoid and which to hit with deadly efficiency because the Jews placed blood from a perfect, unblemished lamb on their doorposts and lintels (Exod 12). Jesus is understood by many Christians to be the perfect blood sacrifice that saves us from similar destruction. God knows to spare the baptized and kill others. Augustine insisted that the virgin birth account had to be literally true because otherwise Mary would have passed sin onto Jesus who therefore would not have met God's requirement for the perfect sacrifice that was needed to silence God's wrath.

Jesus, according to this logic, stands between sinful humanity and a wrathful Deity. Jesus, who taught love of enemies and calls us to live in the presence of God's infinitely compassionate Spirit, is the "Son" of a wrathful God. More ironic still, Jesus as the "Son of Man" or the Lamb,

according to many apocalyptic scenarios, will return as a punishing, violent judge to destroy enemies at the end of history. The idea that God sent Jesus to die for our sins makes sense *if you embrace punishing images of God rejected by Jesus.* An infinitely loving God, who like the prodigal son's father forgives before being asked, doesn't need an atoning sacrifice.

TAKING THE NONVIOLENT STREAM SERIOUSLY: RE-RITUALIZATION

If we take the nonviolent stream of Jesus seriously, then we must re-ritualize communion, or the "Lord's Supper." The Christian tradition generally roots communion in sacrificial and atonement assumptions embedded in the language "this is my body given for you" and "this is my blood shed for you." Fidelity to the nonviolent stream also leads to serious questions about what it means to call Jesus "Savior." From what, we must ask, does Jesus save us? The classic answer is that Jesus saves us from the consequences of our sin. God loved the world so much that God sent Jesus to die for us. If we believe this, then we will not be condemned (John 3:16). Through rose-colored glasses we see a gracious God who loves us enough to send his only son to die in our place so that we might avoid our deserved punishment, go to heaven instead of hell, and have eternal life. But there are brutal images of God, images rejected by Jesus, lurking behind this interpretation. If we believe that Jesus died for us so that we will not be condemned then we should ask, "Condemned by whom?" The answer is God. What remains unstated in classic Christian statements of faith is that Jesus dies in order to save us from God, not from sin, or more accurately, Jesus' sacrificial death saves us from a God who punishes sin. Sin, both personal and social, is often destructive but it is from a punishing God who threatens us with hell that we seek protection. The fearful images of God that are foundational to such views and to all sacrificial rituals are far removed from the Jesus we encountered in chapter 3.

ALTERNATIVES

We model elements of a re-ritualized tradition in Parts Two and Three of *Worship in the Spirit of Jesus*. The worship settings, music, rituals, and liturgies we offer reflect images of God and expectations of history that are consistent with the Jesus we met in the previous chapters and that make sense to us in light of our religious experience. You will notice six features of this alternative approach.

First, the readings used to frame worship and liturgies include biblical texts and nonbiblical readings consistent with the spirit of Jesus. Truth is not confined to the Bible and other "sacred" texts and is often limited by them. We understand that the Bible offers competing and irreconcilable portraits of God, and we choose not to reinforce or reference violent images of God that conflict with Jesus. We don't assume that because something is in the Bible it is true. We don't believe the voice of Matthew's or Luke's Jesus is always consistent with what Jesus said, did, or thought. And we don't assume that attempts within the lectionary to connect Hebrew scriptural passages, the Psalms, New Testament, and Gospel readings bear healthy fruit. As often as not, they reinforce false notions of continuity between Jesus and many violent images of God he rejected. We also believe that the Jesus we meet in chapter 3 can inform but not substitute for our own religious experience. We seek to build on the nonviolent stream associated with Jesus by lifting up engaged Christian and non-Christian voices that inspire us, fictional and nonfictional writings that challenge us, and excerpts from magazines, newspapers, and other sources that help us connect to our world.

Second, the focus of the worship settings, music, and liturgies is on the presence of God in ordinary times and places and in the ordinary spaces of our lives. A linear conception of time and history informs much of the Christian tradition. The Bible moves from chaos, to good creation, to disastrous fall, after which the desperate search to reconcile humanity with God proceeds in earnest. Nothing works until Jesus. His atoning sacrifice satisfies God's wrath, but ironically we await Jesus' second coming and wrathful judgment at the end of the world. The linear view also includes movement from this life to a heavenly realm. This linear view offers little encouragement for us to focus attention on the miracles of lilies and mustard seeds. Jesus spoke of mindfulness and attention to the present. The liturgies seek to cultivate mindfulness in the spirit of Jesus.

Third, the worship settings, music, rituals, and liturgies use a variety of new names and metaphors for God and do not use violent images. Frequently the biblical names and metaphors for God and conceptions of God's power encountered in worship are overwhelmingly patriarchal, and so we experiment with alternatives and encourage you to do so as well. These resources for worship use names and metaphors for God that come from contemporary human experience, shed light on our world, and enrich our religious experience.

Fourth, the worship settings and liturgies do not include prayers of petition because Jesus shows us that God is not a divine puppeteer who controls all events. We affirm and celebrate Jesus' vision of God's power as invitational rather than coercive. Our prayers consist of lifting up to the community our joys, sorrows, pain, concerns, and the state of the world in the context of Jesus' invitation to work for justice, embrace nonviolence, make peace, heal, welcome, serve, and embody authentic life.

Fifth, the worship settings and liturgies do not follow the common order of service in which confession precedes announcement of forgiveness. Jesus says that God is infinitely gracious and forgives us before and without our asking. Instead of asking for and receiving forgiveness, we celebrate mindfulness and the graciousness of God believing that the fruits of mindfulness are joy, compassion, forgiveness, and work for justice.

Finally, communion has been re-ritualized to celebrate real food and community at table, to commit ourselves to working for justice, to be mindful of creation's many gifts, and to embrace our vocation as subversive weeds.

EMBRACING CREATIVE DOUBT

Some people may be uncomfortable with these re-ritualization efforts because they seem to doubt and challenge so much of the tradition. We believe, however, that it is important and necessary to doubt and challenge the violent images of God we have received from the Bible's violent traditions. Jesus certainly did. Here is an imagined informal dialogue between the "doubting Jesus" and his tradition based on the scripture passages we have been studying.

- Our "sacred" text claims that rain is a conditional blessing, but I say to you, based on my experience God provides sunshine and rain to all, the evil and on the good, the righteous and the unrighteous. (Matt 5:45)

- Our "sacred" text claims that God orders us to murder "all who curse father or mother," but I say to you, based on my experience God wants us to challenge oppressive power wherever we see it, including within families. (Luke 12:51–53; Mark 3:31–35)

- Our "sacred" text says those who break Sabbath regulations threaten to bring God's wrath on the nation and should be killed, but I say to you, based on my experience the Sabbath is a gift from a gracious God and civil disobedience is often a requirement of faith. (Mark 2:27; 3:1–6)

- Our "sacred" text says God is God because of superior violence and salvation means defeat of enemies, but I say to you, based on my experience using violence to resist injustice only feeds a spiral of violence. (Mark 12:1–9)

- Our "sacred" text promises we will be recipients of God's preferred violence, but I say to you, based on my experience of God and history this is nothing but a wild and dangerous fantasy. If you want to experience the realm of God, then plant and nourish the mustard seed, become communities of subversive weeds, and embrace the nonviolent, invitational power of God. (Mark 4:30–32)

- Our "sacred" text says that God will come sometime in the near or distant future to establish justice or vindicate the faithful with violence, but I say to you, God is not out there in the sky and the realm of God is not far away or consigned to the Hereafter. God is the Spirit at the heart of life inviting us to new life and the realm is already here in our midst. (Luke 17:20–21)

- Our "sacred" text urges us to hate enemies, but I say to you, based on my experience God encourages us to love enemies and pray for our persecutors because this breaks the spiral of violence and best reflects what God is like. (Matt 5:43–45)

- Our "sacred" text says salvation is the crushing defeat of enemies, but I say to you, based on my experience salvation is healing and restoring all who are excluded to community. We love enemies because that is God's desire and because our enemies are important to our own healing. (Luke 10:30–37)

- Our "sacred" text says I will one day return as the apocalyptic "Son of Man" or "Lamb" to oversee a final judgment in which the good are vindicated and have eternal life and the evil are punished and sentenced to hell, but I say to you, based on my experience this is a betrayal of everything I tried to teach you about life and God. (Luke 15:11–32)

CONCLUSION

As lifelong Christians Bret and I place the nonviolent stream of the Jesus story at the heart of a re-ritualized Christianity (Parts Two and Three) for three reasons. First, we join our voices to many others who in recent years have been engaged in reshaping Christian theology, worship, liturgies, music, and action in light of Jesus, nonviolence, and their own experiences. There are many thousands of efforts, big and small, known and unknown to us, which we have benefited from in important ways.

Second, the nonviolent stream of Jesus feeds us spiritually and speaks to us at the level of our religious experience and our concern for the world. Worship settings, theology, music, and liturgies grounded in the spirit of Jesus inspire us and fill us with wonder, joy, determination, and compassion. They speak to us spiritually, emotionally, and practically as we seek to live authentic lives in a world that is unimaginably beautiful but fracturing under the collective weight of poverty, inequality, injustice, violence, distorted religion, militarization, war, and national arrogance.

Finally, traditional Christian theologies, worship, music, and liturgies that largely ignore the nonviolent stream of Jesus reinforce violent images of God and expectations of history that Jesus rejected and that make little sense to us. We are not waiting for a messiah to save us or for the apocalyptic end. We do not understand human oppression as a punishment from God, nor do we believe that oppressed people should place hope in God's redeeming violence. We believe Jesus shows us how to live, not that God sent Jesus to die for our sins. We embrace Jesus' infinitely loving God and are weary of theologies, music, rituals, and liturgies that express gratitude for the blood sacrifice of Jesus that saves us from the presumed wrath of a punishing Deity. We seek to embrace God's invitation to abundant life and find it difficult to relate to God as the Divine Puppeteer who controls all things and intervenes based on the number and merit of our prayers of petition. We are not preparing for heaven or awaiting Jesus' second coming but seeking to celebrate God's living presence among us. We do not look forward to the violent defeat of our enemies or their permanent punishment in hell but rather we struggle to love enemies and break spirals of violence. We see God in ordinary places and ordinary time. We experience the power of the invitational God in our passion for justice, our concern about violence, our pain and sorrow over poverty, inequality, war, and destruction, our mindfulness of beauty, our embrace of community, our gratitude for music that inspires, our shared meals, our deepest longings, our work for peace, our sense of mystery in creation, our experiments in nonviolence, and in our religious experience of God as the compassionate, invitational Spirit at the heart of all life, inviting us everywhere and always to abundant life.

DISCUSSION

Our Focus: To assess the implications of this material for our worship life and gather ideas and momentum for trying alternatives.

Discuss one or more of the questions in each of the four categories.

Objective Questions

1. What were some of Jesus' doubts about his tradition?

2. What challenges are made here to mainstream Christian tradition and liturgy?

3. What stands out for you about the author's proposed alternative elements of worship?

Reflective Questions

4. How does it make you feel to have the liturgy challenged or questioned?

5. How do you feel about the possibility of abandoning some of the ancient understandings of worship?

6. Do any of the proposed alternatives make you want to say "Amen!"?

7. Do any of the proposed alternatives make you want to say "Forget it!"?

Interpretive Questions

8. What are some of the "different views of Jesus" we get in the New Testament? How does the author resolve these conflicting glimpses of Jesus? How do you resolve these conflicting glimpses?

9. The author points out that Jesus had some doubts about major elements of his religious tradition. What are some of your own

doubts about your Christian tradition? What ideas are foundational for you about your understanding of Christianity?

10. What is one *verb* that would describe God for you? noun? adjective? image? situation?

Decisional Questions

11. If you could change one small thing in "the way we do things around here," what would it be?

12. Read through the worship services found in Part Two. What is one action you or your group could take concerning these worship services?

ACTIVITY

Lectionary Analysis

If your church uses a lectionary, gather the readings for the upcoming week. Make a note of all the places where the various themes of sacred violence appear. In light of your new understandings about scripture and violence talk about what these readings will mean to you and to your congregation.

Create an Alternative Service

Create an alternative worship service and name the elements you include or delete that are different from your current service. Make note of which of the author's suggestions found on pages 86–88 (if any) you decided to use.

Add Dialog to Other Cartoons

Choose a cartoon from the book, look at it in a small group, and talk about the issues it raises for you personally and for your congregation. Then create some dialog "bubbles" to give some of the characters some spoken lines. Or change it to make it fit with your ideas.

NOTES

1. See Leviticus 26 for a classic statement of this formulation and Psalm 44 and the book of Job for dissenting voices.

2. Walter Wink, *Engaging the Powers: Discernment and Resistance in a World of Domination* (Minneapolis: Fortress Press, 1992), 136.

3. Raymond E. Brown et al, ed., *The Jerome Biblical Commentary* (Englewood Cliffs, N.J.: Prentice-Hall, 1968), 77.

4. *Lutheran Book of Worship* (Minneapolis: Augsburg Publishing House, 1978), 58, 92, 101.

5. *The New Century Hymnal* (Cleveland: Pilgrim Press, 1995), 3, 6, 9.

PART TWO

WORSHIP SERVICES AND SONGS
IN THE NONVIOLENT SPIRIT
OF JESUS

INTRODUCTION TO
PART TWO

MY MOTIVATION

Let me (Bret) start with just a glimpse of my motivation for writing this material. Two years ago I ran into an old friend at a church convention. It was a typical three-day get-together of keynote speeches, plenary sessions, large worships, and workshops. We were standing in the back of a big field house auditorium, having a cup of coffee. "How's it going?" I asked her. "At the moment," she said, "I'm really tired of He He He, Blood Blood Blood, King King King." That summed it up for me. I'm tired. I'm tired of sacred violence, subtle or blatant. I'm tired of the cultural violence of sacred male privilege. And in worship, I'm tired of the translating and editing that goes on inside my head as I try to create an awkward fit with what I believe. I'm tired of the little cringe moments, when something goes by and I hope the kids didn't hear or internalize *that* message. If you've gotten this far in the book, perhaps you're tired too.

WORSHIP WITHOUT VIOLENCE

Many of us — liturgists, worship leaders, pastors, song writers, and lay people — have been uncomfortable with biblical violence for years and have been designing services and prayers that discretely avoid the more blatant of these images. We've already been leaning toward the stream of love and nonviolence and have been writing songs and worship services that strongly favor these themes over the themes of violence and atonement. What hasn't been happening, it seems to me, is naming this discomfort out loud and thinking it all the way through to the more subtle and central parts of the worship. Part One of this book provides a lens to focus on worship without violence.

96

When I look through this lens, however, I don't see many worship services that have taken the next step. Few people have built a worship service from the ground up that contains no images or words of spiritual violence. I think the reason for this lack of nonviolent worship services is that such an endeavor must omit large, central pieces of traditional liturgy. Here we are attempting that next step: to build worship services without images or words of spiritual violence. To do so we have omitted the following elements of traditional Christian liturgies:

1. The Confession as the starting point. While we certainly need to confess our sins to one another and forgive one another, Jesus tells us that God forgives us before we ask. Our liturgy needs a different starting point.

2. The Kyrie ("Lord have mercy"). This prayer suggests that the Lord may choose not to have mercy and instead decide to send down violent punishment. Jesus did not witness to such a God.

3. The exclusive use of the Bible for readings. Reading exclusively from the Bible implies that God's revelation and inspiration ended in 100 c.e. This is a violation of Jesus' view that God is present in the here and now, which means God is constantly revealed through the thoughts and lives of contemporary people.

4. The Bible as the "Word of God" in the narrow sense that every word contains isolated truth. Some passages are just plain wrong-headed. Jesus spent a good deal of his time overturning passages of Hebrew scripture that had been misinterpreted. We, along with Jesus, need to be willing to reject the violence within "sacred texts" and not declare that violence as the "Word of God."

5. Creeds. Rather than unifying, which is their intent, creeds can feel coercive. Focused on the all-powerful God and Jesus' sacrificial death, the traditional creeds omit Jesus' life, his teachings, and his work. We need the freedom to craft new statements of faith and belief that reflect the spirit of Jesus.

6. Petitional prayer style. This prayer style implies that God favors some people's prayers and not others. It implies that good fortune

and harm are God-given. This is certainly not the God Jesus was pointing to.

7. Atonement language, imagery, and ritual. Rejecting the sacred violence of atonement means not using images such as "Lamb," "blood shed for you," "died for your sins," and "personal savior." We have concentrated instead on communion as a time to remember the life and teachings of Jesus.

These omissions come with a loss. The worship services Jack and I have written remove time-honored comfort food from the table. Like most folks, I have some sadness about the idea of omitting or changing portions of the liturgy. These liturgical forms have been used by our ancestors, and by continuing to use them we are tied to the cloud of witnesses of the past. As I now remove them, I have a strong sense of loss. But my sense of relief is greater. Let's step forward.

INVITATION INTO THE NEW

If liturgies are "works of the people," they can be "reworked" by the people. As authors, our goal here is simple: to create worship services that spring from the nonviolent stream within our tradition, services that join the radical witness of Jesus with our own faith journeys, services in which we don't have to do any "translating" in our heads, services with no theological "cringe" moments for us as parents.

So what might a liturgy look like without the elements of sacred violence? Readers may be aware of existing services or service pieces that fit much of the bill. As mentioned in chapter 4, we are offering services that lift up both the nonviolent stream of the Christian tradition and important themes from our own faith journey: a nonviolent compassionate God, the ordinary realm of God, equal sharing, inclusive community, resisting oppression, and healing.

The worship service *Here in This Ordinary Place* embodies a new liturgical outline that has five encounter points, places where we enter these themes more deeply and encounter the invitational loving Spirit. We propose the following elements as the framework for a new liturgy:

1. *The Present Moment.* As we gather, we focus our awareness on the immanent Spirit, being mindful of the present moment.

2. *The Inclusive Community.* We celebrate the ordinary splendor of all gathered, the gift of community, and the call to wider inclusion.

3. *The Real World.* We focus our awareness on the world as it is. This leads us to lives of compassion, nonviolence, and simple pleasures.

4. *Commitment.* We name the source of our unity not as shared religious dogma but as our commitment to justice and following the example of Jesus to counter oppression, build inclusion, and bring healing.

5. *Shared Food.* We remember Jesus, whose dining habits were inclusive and radical. We long for sharing and equality.

Included in Part Two are eight services that use one or more of these encounter point elements. Again, the first worship service, *Here in This Ordinary Place,* is a "full-length" service, a reimagined liturgy with all the elements described above. Of the seven shorter services, most contain only one of the above elements, and are suitable for various occasions in the life of the community.

1. *Here in This Ordinary Place*

2. *The Invitation* (Element 3: The Real World)

3. *Dawn of Creation* (Element 3: The Real World)

4. *The Ordinary Realm of God* (Element 1: The Present Moment)

5. *The Potluck of Abundant Life* (Element 5: Shared Food)

6. *Celebrating and Opening the Community* (Element 2: Inclusive Community)

7. *The Nonviolent Teachings of Jesus* (Element 3: The Real World)

8. *The Open Table* (Element 5: Shared Food)

Following the services we have included in Part Three several worship resources to help in leading discussions (A), creating the services (B–F, H), and presenting them to the congregation (G). Worship planners can use the files on the CD-ROM to lay out the services for printed bulletins. @@

LET'S KEEP TALKING

Here are my hopes for this book. I hope Part One gives folks permission (and a format) to talk out loud about something they haven't had the opportunity or safety to talk about. And I hope the services and songs in Parts Two and Three will be meaningful not because of what is *absent* but because of what is *present*. Finally, I hope the services presented here can be both helpful models and meaningful worship for people whose faith urges them to work for justice and peace; who hear the gentle invitation into abundant lives of inclusion, equality, and joy; who seek worship that more clearly reflects their hopes for a world without violence.

HERE IN THIS ORDINARY PLACE

A LITURGY OF NONVIOLENCE
AND JOYFUL WORK FOR PEACE

Celebrating God's presence: in the present moment, in community, in the real world, and in shared food.

Celebrating our call: to generosity, equality, mindfulness, compassion, and peacemaking.

WELCOME AND INTRODUCTION

We welcome all who gather here for worship. This liturgy will be different, something new for us. Christian liturgies often reflect violent images of God featured prominently in the Bible. While acknowledging the contradictory portraits of Jesus and God found within scripture, we have crafted this liturgy with language and forms in tune with the nonviolent God witnessed to by Jesus, and in harmony with our own religious experience. We lift up a God close at hand. A God already among us, not in grand imperial palaces, but in ordinary places. We open ourselves to the invitational power of God that calls us to be mindful of daily mysteries, to be peacemakers, to embody hope, and to live authentic lives in the midst of our joy-filled, suffering world.

GATHERING SONG

"We Gather Longing" (page 184), or other appropriate song.

EMBRACING THE PRESENT MOMENT

Bell Ringing: three times, followed by a brief silence.

OPENING LITANY

Leader: We gather in the embrace of the Creator, in the memory of Jesus and in the mercy of the Loving Spirit:

All: **It's good to be together.**

Leader: Everyone is welcome to be here:

All: **Amen.**

Leader: This is a gathering of hope:

All: **It's good to be together.**

Leader: We've come here today to drain the pools of despair:

All: **Amen.**

Leader: We are people of peace:

All: **It's good to be together.**

Leader: We're here to puncture a hole in the crankcase of the war machine:

All: **Amen.**

Leader: This is the dawn of creation:

All: **It's good to be together.**

Leader: We are waking up . . . and dreaming:

All: **Amen.**

Leader: God is among us:

All: **It's good to be together.**

Leader: Welcome, everyone:

All: **Amen.**

Leader: Let us pray. Gracious Spirit: We are grateful for this time together. As we light this "Candle to the Present Moment," make us mindful of all the miracles that adorn the plain old ordinary world. Lift the veil from our eyes, that we may know your presence among us and see the sweetness and possibility of now. Amen.

Light a Candle to the Present Moment; brief silence.

Song for the Present Moment

"Here in This Ordinary Place" (page 186).

Or these words may be spoken as follows:

Leader: May we awaken to the presence of God,

All: **here in this ordinary place.**

Leader: May we awaken to the power of love,

All: **here in this ordinary crowd.**

Leader: May we build a neighborhood of justice for all,

All: **now in this ordinary time.**

Leader: May we daily work to build a world at peace,

All: **now with these ordinary hands.**

CELEBRATING THE INCLUSIVE COMMUNITY

Leader: Let us take a moment now to celebrate each other. This is our community — it's wonderful . . . and it's ordinary. We also pause now to remember those who are not here, and those we may have excluded. As we light a "Candle of Community," let us commit ourselves to the inclusive ways of Jesus, who welcomed everyone to the table and in so doing shattered barriers, threatened empires, and renewed lives.

Light a Candle of Community; brief silence.

Prayer of Community

Musical accompaniment, "Flower of Compassion #1" (page 188), begins as the first prayer is spoken.

Leader: Let us pray for this community and the whole human family:

We pray for a heart of compassion, that we may look in each face and see a fellow human deserving of respect....

Verse 1, three times.

Cantor intones; all repeat:

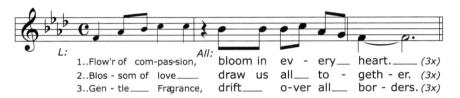

L:
1..Flow'r of com-pas-sion,   bloom in ev - ery__ heart.____ *(3x)*
2..Blos - som of love____   draw us all__ to - geth - er. *(3x)*
3..Gen - tle____ Fragrance,   drift____ o-ver all__ bor - ders. *(3x)*

Leader: We pray for a bond of love, that daily strengthens this community through forgiveness and mutual upbuilding....

Verse 2, three times.

Leader: We pray for a culture of peace that reaches across barriers to include all people....

Verse 3, three times.

Song of Inclusion

"Come Lend Your Beauty to This Place" (page 190), or other appropriate song.

NOTICING THE REAL WORLD

Leader: We turn our hearts now to the world around us:
It is a world of beauty,

All: **and also a world of pain.**

Leader: It's a world of bounty,

All: **and also a world that is unfair and needs healing.**

Leader: God does not parcel out the beauty based on merit,

All: **nor does God mend the brokenness through violent victories.**

Leader: Yet, when our hearts are open, it is a world that invites us to compassion. . . .

Light a Candle to the Real World; brief silence.

Prayer of Mindfulness

Cantor intones; all repeat:

The following lines are read by one or several readers, interspersed with silence and the above refrain ("Make Us Mindful," page 192). Instrumental accompaniment, using the chord pattern of refrain, may continue softly beneath the readings. Read slowly, with plenty of time between lines.

> May we not accumulate wealth while millions are destitute.
> May we not accept membership where others are excluded.
> May we not enjoy privileges given only to some.
> May we open our ears to the call of need.
> May we appreciate what we have and share with others.
> (*Refrain*)
> > May we not walk sightless among miracles.
> > May we notice the ground under our feet.
> > May we not take our days for granted.
> > May we hear birds singing.
> > May we slow down . . . slow down . . . slow down.
> (*Refrain*)
> May we not become cynical in response to injustice.
> May we not tolerate hunger as an acceptable cost of progress.

May we taste what we eat.

May we open our eyes to the signs of the times.

May we embrace the nonviolence of Jesus.

(*Refrain*)

Leader: O God, Desire of Peace, may we truly pay attention to the world as it is, with all its joys and sorrows. In our quieted hearts, may we open to your invitational embrace, which beckons us to fullness of life, where we celebrate beauty and engage the causes of suffering.

All: Amen.

Final refrain — hummed.

Readings, Reflection, and Song

Possible choices for readings include the texts from chapter 3 (pages 50ff. above) or from Resource F (pages 175ff. below). Readings may be followed by a reflection and a song.

PLEDGE OF COMMITMENT

Leader: Friends, we strive to be a community of peacemakers living in the spirit of Jesus. As we light a "Candle of Commitment," let us affirm our commitments to one another and to the great cloud of witnesses who have gone before.

Light a Candle of Commitment, followed by a brief silence.

Say together the following pledge of commitment:

COMMITMENT TO LEARNING THE WAYS OF JESUS

We are united in believing that our faith calls us to act justly in the world. And so we are a community committed to learning: learning what it means to follow the invitation of Jesus to abundant life.

- We are learning to ignore the noisy graffiti of scarcity and fear.

- We are learning to see sufficiency as the end, not the beginning.

- We are learning to give thanks for all that we have and to share it with whoever needs it.

- We are learning to each contribute what we can, aware of our place in the world.

- We are learning to uplift the many who are left out of the earth's uneven abundance.

- We are learning to undo the hoarding of those with wrongful power and privilege.

- We are learning to resist militarism and its corrupting of our national culture.

- We are learning to find joy in savoring rather than consuming.

We will support one another in mutual prayer and dialog as we individually and collectively try to learn these ways.

See Resource E (pages 171ff.) for other pledge of commitment ideas.

THE PRAYERS

Prayers may be either a single printed prayer spoken by all (see Resource C, pages 151ff.), or a time for all to lift up their joys and concerns (see Resource B, 149ff.). In the latter case, proceed as follows:

Cantor intones, all repeat: "Heart of Mercy" (page 193).

Heart of Mer-cy, Heart of Mer-cy, Heart of

Mer-cy, we live in___ you.

Leader: For today's prayer time, rather than petitions, or "request prayers," let us simply lift up names and events, joys and concerns in our lives. After each (or each few), the speaker may say "Heart of Mercy," and all respond, "We live in your love." We now join our hearts and minds in prayer. . . .

Allow time for all to participate, then close with the following:

Closing Prayer

Leader: Heart of Mercy, in silence we listen for your invitation. In silence our hearts open to your way. In silence our spirits melt into one another. As you surround the prayer of our lives, we know that you also hear what is unspoken. And we pray that we too may hear that for one another.

All: Amen.

Final refrain: "Heart of Mercy."

THE SHARED FOOD (COMMUNION)

Transition Song

"The Open Invitation" (page 194), or other appropriate song.

Preface: Remembering the Life of Jesus

Leader: Sharing food is a natural, daily way to build community. As Jesus showed us, sharing food can also be a subversive act that challenges all systems that find hunger acceptable. In this meal,

- we remember the witness of Jesus, who instructed his followers to clothe the naked and feed the hungry,

- we remember Jesus, who showed the power of sharing over hoarding by the feeding of the five thousand,

- we remember Jesus, who defied religious teaching by eating with outcasts and welcoming all to his table.

Light a Candle of Sharing; brief silence.

Blessing the Food

Leader lifts hands to "embrace" the group.

Leader: Everyone is welcome to be here:

All: **In this way, we lift up a world of inclusion, where all people live with respect and dignity.**

Leader lifts the bread into view.

Leader: Everyone present will receive a share:

All: **In this way, we lift up a world of generosity, where, as in the examples of Jesus, abundance overcomes scarcity so that all are fed.**

Leader lifts wine into view.

Leader: Everyone is invited now to take a portion and pass it along:

All: **In this way, we lift up a world of sufficiency, where entrenched systems of privilege are challenged, wealth is shared equally, and all are satisfied with enough.**

Leader: Let us pray: Generous God, as we share food, both now and at home, may it sustain our firm belief in the transforming spirit of nonviolence and love. May it remind us of Jesus' teachings and strengthen us as we journey toward your will of justice and peace.

All: **Amen.**

Serving the Food

Ritual words for Server:

Server: We eat from one loaf. (bread)

We share one cup. (wine)

Songs during Distribution

"Give Us Our Daily Bread" (page 199) and other appropriate songs.

1. Give us our dai-ly bread.   Give us our dai-ly bread.

Give us our dai-ly bread.   May we be sa-tis-fied.

2. May we be satisfied (3x)   3. Never be satisfied (3x)
   With only what we need.   If any be denied.

4. Passing the gift along (3x)
   Each adding as we can.

Postcommunion Litany (optional)

Leader: Jesus taught us these truths:
        The world is filled with good things:

All: may we all share in them equally.

Leader: Sufficiency is the key to abundant life:

All: help yourself and pass it along.

Leader: Food is the gift of the Generous Spirit:

All: thanks be to the Giver.

Leader: We eat from one loaf:

All: make room at the table.

Postcommunion Prayer

Leader: Let us pray. Generous Spirit,

**All: thank you for this food. And thank you for the pleasures
           of eating together. With this meal you have given us both**

strength and hunger: strength for our bodies, strength for our community, and hunger for a world of justice. May we taste these same gifts at every meal. Amen.

Postcommunion Song

"Now, O Spirit" (page 196).

BENEDICTION

Leader: Friends, (let us) go now in joy and service —
Scattering like tiny seeds.
Trusting that you (we) are in the right place.
Rooting in the Soil of Infinite Love.
Accepting the Invitation to emerge.
Breaking up the pavement of war and oppression.
And blooming in joyful bunches.

All: **We are the irrepressible weeds of peace. Amen.**

SENDING SONG

"Little by Little" (page 198), or other appropriate song.

Note: to create a second setting for this service, substitute a new set of songs as follows:

Gathering Song: "Let All Hearts Unite" (page 203) replaces "We Gather Longing."

Song for the Present Moment: "May We Awaken" (page 208) replaces "Here in This Ordinary Place."

Prayer of Community: "Flower of Compassion #2" (page 202) replaces "Flower of Compassion #1."

Song of Inclusion: "Stream of Mercy Never Failing" (page 212) or "A Dazzling Bouquet" (page 220) replaces "Come Lend Your Beauty to This Place."

Prayer of Mindfulness: "Listen" (page 206) or "O Compassion" (page 209) replaces "Make Us Mindful."

Song during Distribution: "Give Us Today" (page 200) replaces "Give Us Our Daily Bread."

Sending Song: "O God, You Will Show Us the Path of Life" (page 210) replaces "Little by Little."

SERVICE 2

THE INVITATION

SHORT SERVICE OF SOCIAL CONCERNS
AND ACTION (20–30 MINUTES)

Liturgical Element 3: The Real World

Note to worship planner: It will be best to have several readers for this service. They can alternate in reading not only the litany but also the headlines and short readings. Also, in advance, be sure to gather headlines from local and regional papers (see Resource D, pages 154ff. for details).

The source for each of the quotations in these services is located at the end of Resource D on pages 163–170.

INTRODUCTION

Welcome. Our worship today lifts up our desire to follow the ways of Jesus, who lived his life challenging injustice, engaging in the problems of the day, and acting with compassion. In our prayers, our readings, our song, and our silence, we are invited to ponder deeply the invitation of the Spirit to respond to our world with lives of compassion. We begin now in silence.

Allow a brief silence, and then begin as follows.

SONG

"We Gather Longing" (page 184), two or three verses.

OPENING LITANY

Leader: In hope, in longing:

All: We're glad to come together.

113

Leader: In forgiveness, and in community:

All: We're glad to come together.

Leader: In many moods, in many shapes:

All: We're glad to come together.

Leader: In many sizes and many colors:

All: We're glad to come together.

Leader: In peace, in joy:

All: We're glad to come together.

Leader: In trust, in loveliness:

All: We're glad to come together.

Leader: In solidarity with those who struggle:

All: We're glad to come together.

Leader: In resistance to those who dominate:

All: We're glad to come together.

Leader: In memory of Jesus, who lived with compassion:

All: We're glad to come together.

Leader: In memory of all who act with courage:

All: We're glad to come together.

Leader: In assurance that we belong here:

All: We're glad to come together.

Leader: In the presence of Mercy Unbounded:

All: We're glad to come together.

Leader: Let us pray:
Remind us, O Spirit, that life is worth living. Remind us, O Creator, that the struggle for justice is worth undertaking. Remind us, O Mercy, that love and action are one. Guide us by

Jesus' life, that we cast cynicism aside, that we walk with joy and determination, that we unfold our hands and get them dirty.

All: **Amen.**

SONG

"Where There Is Hatred" (page 216), verse 1, two times.

LISTENING TO THE INVITATION

Using the following as a template, intersperse short readings with a sung refrain and time for silent reflection, perhaps underscored with light accompaniment on guitar or keyboard. Adjust the number of readings to the time available. Use a gentle pace throughout, allowing time to slow down.

Leader: Jesus said, be compassionate as God is compassionate. He empowered the poor and outcasts. He challenged the powerful. He showed that the realm of God is among us, that abundant life is possible, if only we would pay attention. Let us pause now to consider our call to compassion, to listen in prayer and silence to the invitation of the Spirit.

Silence.

Refrain: *"O Compassion" (page 209).*

O Compassion. In the quiet of my heart, waken me.

Those who say religion has nothing to do with politics do not know what religion means. — MAHATMA GANDHI

Headlines: Read one or two newspaper headlines.

Unrolling the scroll, Jesus found the place where it is written: God has anointed me to preach the good news to the poor, to proclaim release to the captives and recovering of sight to the blind; to set at liberty those who are oppressed, to proclaim the acceptable year of Yahweh. — LUKE 4:17–19, PARAPHRASE

Headlines: Read one or two newspaper headlines.

What good is it to me if Mary gave birth to Jesus 1400 years ago if I do not also give birth to him in my time and my culture?

— MEISTER ECKHART

Headlines: Read one or two newspaper headlines.

Silence.

Refrain: *"O Compassion"* (page 209).

O Compassion. In the quiet of my heart, waken me.

But a Samaritan on the road was moved with compassion when he saw this victim. He went up to him and bandaged his wounds, pouring oil and wine on them. Then he lifted him up to his own donkey, carried him to the inn, and looked after him. . . . Go and do the same yourself.   — LUKE 10:33–35, 37, PARAPHRASE

In the face of suffering, one has no right to turn away. . . . In the face of injustice, one may not look the other way. . . . To watch over a man that grieves is a more urgent duty than to think of God.

— ELIE WIESEL

Headlines: Read one or two newspaper headlines.

I stressed the need for a social gospel to supplement the gospel of individual salvation. I suggested that only a "dry as dust" religion prompts a minister to extol the glories of heaven while ignoring the social conditions that cause people an earthly hell. . . . I asked how *our people* would ever gain *their* freedom without the guidance, support, and inspiration of *their* spiritual leaders.

— MARTIN LUTHER KING JR., ABOUT SPEAKING
TO A GROUP OF MINISTERS, PARAPHRASE

Headlines: Read one or two newspaper headlines.

Refrain: *"O Compassion"* (page 209).

O Compassion. In the quiet of my heart, waken me.

When we are mindful, touching deeply the present moment, we can see and listen deeply, and the fruits are always understanding, acceptance, love, and the desire to relieve suffering and bring joy.

— THICH NHAT HANH

Headlines: Read one or two newspaper headlines.

Silence.

Refrain: "*O Compassion*" (page 209).

O Compassion. In the quiet of my heart, waken me.

Conclude with a prayer:

Leader: Infinite Compassion,

All: **waken our hearts, that we engage the causes of suffering and celebrate small miracles. Amen.**

SONG

"*Where There Is Hatred*" (page 216), *verses 2 and 3.*

CLOSING PRAYER

Leader: Let us pray: Remind us, O Spirit, that life is worth living. Remind us, O Creator, that the struggle for justice is worth undertaking. Remind us, O Mercy, that love and action are one. Guide us by Jesus' life, that we cast cynicism aside, that we walk with joy and determination, that we unfold our hands and get them dirty.

All: **Amen.**

CLOSING SONG

"*We Shall Be Peace*" (page 214).

DAWN OF CREATION

MORNING WORSHIP (20–30 MINUTES)

Liturgical Element 3: The Real World

Note to worship planner: It will be best to have several readers for this service. These folks can alternate in reading not only the litany but also the overlapping readings of the lists of creatures. In advance, you will need to gather one or more lists of local flora and fauna, or other natural wonders. (see Resource D, pages 156ff. for details). Before the service, divide the list into six to eight pieces, about twenty-five items in each part. Give these sublists to six to eight readers and instruct them how and when to read these out loud. The readings should not be regimented and orderly but spaced at random and overlapping — for three minutes.

INTRODUCTION

Welcome to this service. Today we will celebrate the beauty and majesty of all creation, the ongoing and ever-blooming creating spirit of God. We will worship with short songs, readings, and prayers. The readings will be sometimes separate, sometimes overlapped with one another. Our silence too will be our prayer, prayer for mindfulness of the miracles of today. Let us enter now into worship and prayer.

OPENING SONG

"Here in This Ordinary Place" (page 186), verse 1 and chorus.

OPENING LITANY

Leader: Sisters and Brothers, as we wake and gather together:

All: **may our eyes be opened.**

Leader: Here in this ordinary room:

All: **may our eyes be opened.**

Leader: Here in this sacred moment:

All: **may our eyes be opened.**

Leader: Here at the dawn of creation:

All: **may our eyes be opened.**

Leader: The Creator is busy right now:

All: **may our eyes be opened.**

Leader: This place is filled with good things:

All: **may our eyes be open.**

PRAYER

Leader: The days pass and the years vanish,
and we walk sightless among miracles.
Creator, fill our eyes with seeing
and our minds with knowing;
Let there be moments
when the candles of your Presence
illumine the darkness in which we walk.

— GATES OF PRAYER, PARAPHRASE

All: **As the sun rises each day in perfect newness,
so may we break upon each new day
with splendor and expectation:
renewed creatures content with reflected radiance
and dirty fingernails. Amen.**

Brief silence.

SONG

"Here in This Ordinary Place" (page 186), verse 1 and chorus.

THE CREATIVE WORDS OF GOD

Using the following as a template, read aloud lists of created life, interspersed with a sung refrain and time for silent reflection. Below we use three lists — birds, plants, and people. Adjust the number of lists you use to the time available. Use a gentle pace throughout, allowing time to slow down.

Leader: How filled with awe is this place:

All: and we did not know it.

Repeat three times, pause between each.

LIST 1: THE BIRDS

Refrain

"Web of Beauty" (page 215).

Short Reading

Leader: A Reading from Hildegard of Bingen:
        Glance at the sun. See the moon and the stars.
        Gaze at the beauty of earth's greenings. Now, think.
        What delight God gives to humankind with all these things.

Announcement

Leader: The word goes forth from the mouth of God:

All: and does not return empty.

Leader: Every creature is a word of God,

All: and all creation is a book about God.

                                    — ISA 55 AND MEISTER ECKHART

The Creative Words #1: "A reading from the book of birds of Minnesota . . ." (see page 157 for a sample list)

Readers now call out the species names into the air in no given order and some overlapping. Conclude with the following couplet or omit and allow silence.

Leader: This is the word of the Creator:

All: **Thanks be to God.**

LIST 2: THE WILDFLOWERS

Refrain

"Web of Beauty" (page 215).

Short Readings

> Notice how the wild lilies grow: They don't slave and they never spin. Yet let me tell you, even Solomon at the height of his glory was never decked out like one of them.
>
> — MATT 6:28–29, PARAPHRASE

> What is the test that you have indeed undergone this holy birth? Listen carefully. If this birth has truly taken place within you, then every single creature points you toward God.
>
> — MEISTER ECKHART

Announcement

Leader: The word goes forth from the mouth of God:

All: **and does not return empty.**

Leader: Every creature is a word of God,

All: **and all creation is a book about God.**

The Creative Words #2: "A reading from the book of wildflowers of Minnesota..." (see page 160 for a sample list)

As above, prearrange to have six to eight people each have a list of twenty-five species names, and read out loud at random and overlapping for three minutes. Conclude with the following couplet or omit and allow silence.

Leader: This is the word of the Creator:

All: **Thanks be to God.**

LIST 3: THE PEOPLE

Refrain

"*Web of Beauty*" *(page 215).*

Short Reading

Leader: A Reading from Meister Eckhart:
God is creating the entire universe
fully and totally in this present now.
Everything God created in the beginning —
and even previous to that . . .
God creates now all at once.

Announcement

Leader: The word goes forth from the mouth of God:

All: and does not return empty.

Leader: Every creature is a word of God,

All: and all creation is a book about God.

The Creative Words #3: "A reading from the book of names of the people here . . . "

As before, prearrange to have six to eight people reading lists of names of those present, if possible. Conclude with the following couplet or omit and allow silence.

Leader: This is the word of the Creator:

All: Thanks be to God.

Silence.

SONG

"*Yea, O God*" *(page 218).*

CLOSING PRAYER

Leader: The days pass and the years vanish,
and we walk sightless among miracles.
Creator, fill our eyes with seeing
and our minds with knowing;
Let there be moments
when the candles of your Presence
illumine the darkness in which we walk.

All: **As the sun rises each day in perfect newness,**
So may we break upon each new day
with splendor and expectation.
Renewed creatures content with reflected radiance
and dirty fingernails. Amen.

SENDING SONG

"Yea, O God" (page 218), reprise.

SERVICE 4

THE ORDINARY REALM OF GOD
ADJUSTING OUR EXPECTATIONS (25 MINUTES)
Liturgical Element 1: The Present Moment

INTRODUCTION

Welcome to worship today. Our service is focused on Jesus' teachings concerning the realm of God. People were expecting a mighty victory, but Jesus said it would be quite different, commonplace, and already in fact present. Through our prayers, song, readings, and silence, we pray that our hearts and minds be opened to this ever-present realm of God. We begin in silence.

OPENING SONG

"We Gather Longing" (page 184), three verses.

OPENING LITANY

Leader: Welcome.
We have come here today from our many busy lives:

All: may we slow down now and pay attention.

Leader: Our thoughts are full of to-do lists:

All: may we slow down now and pay attention.

Leader: Our lives are packed with good things:

All: may we slow down now and pay attention.

Leader: Some of us are bursting with exciting news:

All: may we slow down now and pay attention.

Leader: Some of us are burdened with sadness:

All: **may we slow down now and pay attention.**

Leader: We're seeking and building a community of hope:

All: **may we slow down now and pay attention.**

Leader: What we're after may be closer than we think:

All: **may we slow down now and pay attention.**

Leader: The spirit of love is among us always:

All: **may we slow down now and pay attention.**

Leader: Let us pray: Ever-present God, Beauty Taken for Granted,

All: **may we attune our senses to what is often overlooked. May we pay attention to each moment, notice that which is present, treat the commonplace as important, and respond to your invitation. Amen.**

SONG

"May We Awaken" (page 208), verse 1, cantor only.

GOD'S REALM IS OUR PLACE

Using several readers, alternate the following readings with song and silence. Adjust the number of readings as time allows.

Leader: When we look at the world around us, we are often troubled and frustrated by the prevalence of evil and oppression. It seems that our work to the contrary is for naught. Throughout history, people have longed for divine intervention and a convincing, mighty victory of right over wrong. Jesus, however, pointed us in quite a different direction.

Refrain: *"May We Awaken" (page 208), verse 1, all.*

With what can we compare God's realm, or what parable will we use for it? It is like a mustard seed, which, when sown upon the ground, is the smallest of all the seeds on earth; yet when it is sown it grows up and becomes the greatest of shrubs, and puts forth large branches, so that the birds can make nests in its shade.

— JESUS, IN MARK 4:30–32, PARAPHRASE

The mustard plant is dangerous even when domesticated in the garden and it is deadly when growing wild in the grain fields. And those nesting birds, which may strike us as charming, represented to ancient farmers a permanent danger to the seed and the grain. The point, in other words, is not just that the mustard plant starts as a proverbially small seed and grows into a shrub of three, four, or even more feet in height. It is that it tends to take over where it is not wanted, that it tends to get out of control, and that it tends to attract birds within cultivated areas, where they are not particularly desired. And that, says Jesus, was what the Kingdom was like. Like a pungent shrub with dangerous take-over properties.

— JOHN DOMINIC CROSSAN

Once Jesus was asked by the Pharisees when God's realm was coming, and he answered, "It is not coming with things that can be observed; nor will they say, 'Look, here it is!' or 'There it is!' For in fact, it is already among you."

— JESUS, IN LUKE 17:20–21, PARAPHRASE

Refrain: *"May We Awaken"* (page 208), verse 2, all.

The realm of God "is already breaking into the world, and it comes, not as an imposition from on high, but as the leaven slowly causing the dough to rise."   — WALTER WINK

. . . the time is always ripe to do right. Now is the time to make real the promise of democracy and transform our pending national elegy into a creative psalm of *humanity*. Now is the time to lift our national policy from the quicksand of racial injustice to the solid rock of human dignity.   — MARTIN LUTHER KING JR., PARAPHRASE

Refrain: *"May We Awaken"* (page 208), verse 3, all.

Friend, hope for the Guest while you are alive.
Jump into experience while you are alive!
Think...and think...while you are alive.
What you call "salvation" belongs to the time before death.
If you don't break your ropes while you are alive,
Do you think
Ghosts will do it after?
The idea that the soul will join with the ecstatic
Just because the body is rotten —
That is all fantasy.
What is found now is found then.
If you find nothing now,
You will simply end up with an apartment in the city of Death
If you make love with the divine now, in the next life
You will have the face of satisfied desire.   — KABIR

The time has come.
The realm of God is near.   — JESUS, IN MARK 1:15, PARAPHRASE

In music, in the sea, in a flower, in a leaf, in an act of kindness.
...I see what people call God in all these things.
                                        — PABLO CASALS

Nobody sees a flower, really — it is so small it takes time — we
haven't time — and to see takes time, like to have a friend takes
time.   — GEORGIA O'KEEFFE

Silence.

CONVERSATION

Leader: Turn to someone now and talk about what has come up for you
during this time of reflection — something that has caught your
attention as you sit here.

SONG

"O God, You Will Show Us the Path of Life" (page 210), *verses 1 and 2.*

BENEDICTION

Leader: In leaving, be certain: the realm of God is among us, ordinary
and inconspicuous. It is cropping up everywhere, wanted or not.
Let us encourage each other in the coming days to see, to live
in, and to be the realm of God. Like weeds in the cracks, may
we joyfully break up the concrete.

All: Amen.

CLOSING SONG

"O God, You Will Show Us the Path of Life" (page 210) verses 3 and 4.

THE POTLUCK OF ABUNDANT LIFE
VERY SHORT SERVICE (10 MINUTES)
FOLLOWED BY A LONG POTLUCK

Liturgical Element 5: Shared Food

Worship Note: Any of the various readings in this service may be done by a single person or the entire group.

INTRODUCTION

Welcome, everyone. Before we eat we'd like to take about ten minutes to have a song, a prayer, and a dedication for the potluck. A potluck is not only a great way to eat, but also a concrete demonstration of what we value in our lives: equality, inclusion of all, compassion, and generosity. Let us now express together our gratitude to God and our commitment to the teachings of Jesus.

CANTOR

"The Open Invitation" (page 194), verse 1, solo, slowly.

ANNOUNCEMENT

Leader: From before the dawn of time to beyond the sunset of days,
The Creating Spirit rings like a dinner bell,
calling everything to the banquet of being.
And in this moment, like all moments, the bell is ringing.
It's the welcome call to join the potluck of abundant living.
We are here because, for today, we have heard the bell
and gladly accept the invitation.

SONG

"The Open Invitation" (page 194), verses 1, 4–6, up tempo.

WE REMEMBER

Leader: As Jesus taught us, abundant life is intended for all. It spreads
as we practice equality, compassion/nonviolence, generosity,
and inclusive community. May this potluck remind us of our
commitment to these ways. Today we lift up in particular the
practice of _____ [*inclusive community, generosity, equality, or
compassion/nonviolence*]. *Name one, then light a candle and read
aloud the corresponding section below.*

Inclusive Community: Eating together builds our community. We
look around and enjoy the look of our community, not a world of
fashion models and superstars, but ordinary people in all our ordinary
splendor. We remember Jesus, who ate with outcasts as well as friends.
Eating was for him an act of inclusion. We pause to remember those
not here, and those we have neglected to make welcome. *(pause)*

We commit ourselves to building an inclusive community here
and now. We know that this involves resisting strong forces that try
to keep some people out because of their skin color, income level,
affectional orientation, physical shape, etc. We strive to resist with
nonviolence. In this meal, where everyone is welcome, let us renew
our commitment to building a world where all are included.

Generosity: We have each brought what we can to share at this
meal; this is a small response to the limitless Generosity beneath all
life. We are thankful for the riches of the earth, not scarce and held
back per our behavior, but freely and carelessly given by the spirit. It
is this same generosity that guides our living. We know that gratitude
and forgiveness can be overshadowed by forces of selfishness and
vengeance. We strive to resist these forces, as Jesus did, nonviolently.
Everyone who comes can eat tonight, whether or not they brought
food. With this small gesture, we renew our commitment to build a
society based on generosity rather than greed.

Equality: As we dish up our plates, we keep one eye on those in line behind us. We know that others have not yet been served, and we dish up accordingly. In this way, we are mindful of our desire for lives of sufficiency, where the world's resources are equally divided and all have decent lives. We are mindful of Jesus' invitation to abundance, rooted in enough for all. We know that building this world of fairness involves resisting strong forces that try to protect the rich and powerful. We strive to resist these forces with persistence and nonviolent ingenuity. In this meal, we celebrate our commitment to building a world of equality and justice.

Compassion: Eating together involves talking around tables. Our conversations inform us about what's happening in the community. Some of what's happening is wonderful; some of it is tragic. We tell each other what we know; and we listen and learn. Nothing is left out of our gabbing. Jesus reminds us that this life is important — our lives, our times, our present world — and that we are to remain mindful of everything around us. We know there are strong forces that lead us to forget what's happening in our lives, to ignore what our bodies tell us, to believe a false picture of what's happening in the world, to escape into a pretend world where all is happy and easy, where difficult problems are resolved with violence. We resist these forces with honest chatter. In this meal, our conversation is our mindfulness and leads us to honesty, joy, and compassionate action.

INVITATION

Leader: All are welcome. Don't worry about whether you brought anything; there will be enough for all.

All: Amen.

TABLE GRACE

Sung or spoken, either a familiar one or perhaps "Give Us Today" (page 200).

SERVICE 6

CELEBRATING AND OPENING THE COMMUNITY

SERVICE OF UNBOUNDED WELCOME
(30 MINUTES)

Liturgical Element 2: The Inclusive Community

INTRODUCTION

Welcome, everyone. Our worship today includes songs, prayers, readings, and silence. Through many voices and many images of God, we lift up the teachings of Jesus regarding welcoming the stranger and the outcast. His open table, a threat to many, is an invitation to us to do likewise. We pray now together that we may learn to follow.

GATHERING SONG

"Let All Hearts Unite" (page 203), verses 1–3.

COMMUNITY LITANY

Leader: Sisters and brothers,
As we gather here now:

All: may our hearts be joined in love.

Leader: Here in this ordinary crowd:

All: may our hearts be joined in love.

Leader: In this ordinary time:

All: may our hearts be joined in love.

Leader: We remember those not here:

All: **may our hearts be joined in love.**

Leader: We remember those excluded:

All: **may our hearts be joined in love.**

Leader: We remember Jesus' open invitations:

All: **may our hearts be joined in love.**

Leader: We are meant for community:

All: **may our hearts be joined in love.**

Leader: We are bound for reconciliation:

All: **may our hearts be joined in love.**

Leader: The Loving Spirit is among us:

All: **may our hearts be joined in love.**

Leader: Let us pray: God, Flower of Compassion: you bloom in every heart. You draw us to one another in kindness and mutual forgiveness. You fire us with the joy of companionship. Forgive our failures to include the outcasts. Lead us now beyond the borders of comfort and convenience to true community, uniting us with those from lands and lives quite distant from our own.

All: **Amen.**

SONG

"Stream of Mercy Never Failing" (page 212), verses 1 and 2, or "A Dazzling Bouquet" (page 220).

OPENING UP TO A DEEPER, WIDER COMMUNITY

Using the following as a template, intersperse the readings with silence and a short refrain — "Flower of Compassion #2" (page 202). Adjust the length and number of readings as time allows.

Leader: Let us pray now for a heart of compassion, that we may look in each face and see a fellow human deserving of respect...

Cantor: Flower of Compassion,

All: bloom within, bloom within, bloom within, each heart.

Whatever God does, the first outburst is always compassion.
                                          — MEISTER ECKHART

Be you compassionate, as your Creator is compassionate.
                                — JESUS, IN LUKE 6:36, PARAPHRASE

Every act of love is a work of peace, no matter how small. The fruit
of love is service. The fruit of service is peace.   — MOTHER TERESA

God is love.   I JOHN 4:8

Leader: We pray for a bond of love that daily strengthens this community
        through forgiveness and mutual upbuilding. . . .

Cantor: Blossom of Love, you

All: draw us close, draw us close, draw us close together.

When I can no longer bear my loneliness, I take it to my friends. For
I must share it with all the friends of God. "Do you suffer?" "So do I!"
                                — MECHTILD OF MAGDEBURG

Joy was in fact the most characteristic result of all Jesus' activity
amongst the poor and the oppressed.   — ALBERT NOLAN

I am human. Nothing human is alien to me.
              — ROMAN PLAYWRIGHT TERENCE, SECOND CENTURY B.C.E.

Leader: We pray for a culture of peace and inclusion that reaches across
        barriers to embrace all people. . . .

Cantor: Delicate fragrance,

All: drift beyond, drift beyond, drift beyond, all borders.

Air, blowing everywhere, serves all creatures.
                                          — HILDEGARD OF BINGEN

You have heard that it was said, "You shall love your neighbor and hate your enemy." But I say to you, love your enemies and pray for those who persecute you, so that you may be children of God in heaven; for God makes the sun rise on the evil and on the good, and sends rain on the righteous and on the unrighteous.

— MATT 5:43–45, PARAPHRASE

There was a man going from Jerusalem down to Jericho when he fell into the hands of robbers. They stripped him, beat him up, and left him half dead by the roadside. Now by coincidence a priest was going down that road; when he caught sight of the man, he went out of his way to avoid him. In the same way, when a Levite came to the place, he took one look at the man and crossed the road to avoid him. But this Samaritan who was traveling that way came to where the man was and was moved to pity at the sight of him. He went up to him and bandaged his wounds, pouring olive oil and wine on them. He hoisted him onto his own animal, brought him to an inn, and looked after him. . . . Go and do likewise.

— JESUS, IN LUKE 10:30–34, 37, PARAPHRASE

I'm not into isms and asms. There isn't a Catholic moon and a Baptist sun. I know the universal God is universal. . . . I feel that the same God-force that is the mother and father of the pope is the mother and father of the loneliest wino on the planet.

— DICK GREGORY

Cantor: Flower of Compassion,

All: bloom within, bloom within, bloom within every heart.

BEYOND OUR BORDERS: NAMING THE INCLUSIVE COMMUNITY

Leader: As we desire inclusive community, we pause to remember now those who are excluded. Excluded from power, from privilege, from comfort in our society. Excluded by our actions, and the actions of others. Not made welcome. We name them aloud and in our hearts. . . .

After allowing time, conclude with a prayer.

Leader: God, Flower of Compassion: you bloom in every heart. You draw
us to one another in kindness and mutual forgiveness. You fire
us with the joy of companionship. Forgive our failures to include
the outcasts. Lead us now beyond the borders of comfort and
convenience to true community, uniting us with those from
lands and lives quite distant from our own.

All: Amen.

SONG

"Stream of Mercy Never Failing" (page 212), verses 3 and 4.

BENEDICTION

Leader: Go now in joy, building, living in, and enjoying a community full
of welcome and equality.

All: Thanks be to God.

CLOSING SONG

*"Let All Hearts Unite" (page 203), verses 1, 4, 5, 6. If it is late evening, use
"Turn My Heart to Peace" (page 207).*

THE NONVIOLENT TEACHINGS OF JESUS

SHORT SERVICE OF READING AND REFLECTION (25 MINUTES)

Liturgical Element 3: The Real World

INTRODUCTION

Welcome to worship. Our theme for today is nonviolence for Jesus and ourselves. Jesus taught us that God, and the realm of God, is quite different from what most believers are expecting. Jesus taught us that God is nonviolent and all compassionate — and already among us in the joys and sorrows of the real world. In this short service, we take time to hear his words and ponder their meaning for us. Let us begin in silence.

SONG

"Let All Hearts Unite" (page 203), verses 1–4.

OPENING LITANY

Leader: Welcome, everyone.
Let us gather in prayer and compassion.

All: It's good to be here.

Leader: Jesus invites us now
. . . to pay deep attention to the world around us:

All: We pray with our eyes.

Leader: . . . to hear the sounds of creation:

All: We pray with our ears.

Leader: ... to feel the pain of our fellow people:

All: We pray with our hearts.

Leader: ... to taste the joy of new life:

All: We pray with our smiles.

Leader: ... to smell the banquet of abundance for all:

All: We pray with our appetites.

Leader: This world is our home.

All: We pray with our lives.

Leader: Let us pray now with words:

> O God, Blossom of Love, give us courage and an open spirit as we consider the life and teachings of Jesus. In our prayer, in our silence, and in our conversations, may we feel your invitational embrace beckoning us to fullness of life, where we celebrate beauty and engage the causes of suffering. **Amen.**

REFRAIN

"Listen" (page 206). Repeat verses 5–6 several times.

READING AND REFLECTION

Read aloud, and invite someone to reflect on, one of the passages in Part One, chapter 3.

SONG

"Let's Leave Our Fears and Comforts Now" (page 204), or other song appropriate to the shared word.

CLOSING LITANY

Leader: Let us go out in prayer and compassion.

All: It's good to return to our daily lives.

Leader: The spirit of Jesus invites us now
              ... to pay deep attention to the world around us:

All: **We will pray with our eyes.**

Leader: . . . to hear the sounds of creation:

All: **We will pray with our ears.**

Leader: . . . to feel the pain of our fellow people:

All: **We will pray with our hearts.**

Leader: . . . to taste the joy of new life:

All: **We will pray with our smiles.**

Leader: . . . to smell the banquet of abundance for all:

All: **We will pray with our appetites.**

Leader: This world is our home.

All: **We will pray with our lives.**

Leader: Let us pray with words:
O God, Blossom of Love, give us courage and an open spirit as we consider the life and teachings of Jesus. In our silence and through our senses, may we feel your invitational embrace beckoning us to fullness of life, where we celebrate beauty and engage the causes of suffering.

All: **Amen.**

CLOSING SONG

"O God, You Will Show Us the Path of Life" (page 210).

SERVICE 8

THE OPEN TABLE

SHORT SERVICE WITH COMMUNION
(25 MINUTES)

Liturgical Element 5: Shared Food

INTRODUCTION

Welcome to today's communion service. This communion ritual will have a different emphasis from the traditional one. Rather than remembering Jesus' death, we will use this meal as an opportunity to remember his life and teachings: his inclusion of outcasts and strangers, his insistence on abundance over scarcity, his call to generosity, and his challenge to systems of greed. In song, prayer, and shared food, let us now celebrate the way of Jesus.

GATHERING SONG

"Here in This Ordinary Place" (page 186), verse 1 only, or other gathering song.

OPENING LITANY

Begin with "Please repeat after me":

Leader: We gather together

All: **We gather together**

Leader: In the name of Jesus

All: **In the name of Jesus**

Leader: The lover of enemies

All: **The lover of enemies**

Leader: Who welcomed the stranger

All: **Who welcomed the stranger**

Leader: Who dined with outcasts

All: **Who dined with outcasts**

Leader: Who healed the sick

All: **Who healed the sick**

Leader: Who challenged the powerful

All: **Who challenged the powerful**

Leader: Who called for compassion

All: **Who called for compassion**

Leader: Who showed that God is love

All: **Who showed that God is love**

Leader: We gather here now

All: **We gather here now**

Leader: In the name of Jesus

All: **In the name of Jesus**

Leader: Let us pray. Gracious Spirit:

All: **We are grateful for this time together. As we gather, lift the veil from our eyes, that we may know your presence among us and live as Jesus taught, finding abundance through joyful habits of sharing, generosity, justice, and hospitality. Amen.**

SHARED FOOD (COMMUNION)

Transition Song

"The Open Invitation" (page 194), or other appropriate song.

Preface: Remembering the Life of Jesus

Leader: Sharing food is a natural, daily way to build community. As
Jesus showed us, sharing food can also be a subversive act
that challenges all systems that find hunger acceptable. In
this meal, we remember the witness of Jesus, who instructed
his followers to clothe the naked and feed the hungry ... who
showed the power of sharing over hoarding by the feeding of the
five thousand ... who defied religious teaching by eating with
outcasts and welcoming all to his table.

Light a Candle of Sharing; brief silence.

Blessing the Food

Leader lifts hands to "embrace" the group.

Leader: Everyone is welcome to be here:

**All: In this way, we lift up a world of inclusion, where all people
live with respect and dignity.**

Leader lifts the bread into view.

Leader: Everyone present will receive a share:

**In this way, we lift up a world of generosity, where, as in the
examples of Jesus, abundance overcomes scarcity so that all
are fed.**

Leader lifts the wine into view.

Leader: Everyone is invited now to take a portion and pass it along:

**All: In this way, we lift up a world of sufficiency, where entrenched
systems of privilege are challenged, wealth is shared equally,
and all are satisfied with enough.**

Leader: Let us pray: Generous God, as we share food, both now and at
home, may it sustain our firm belief in the transforming spirit
of nonviolence and love. May it remind us of Jesus' teachings

and strengthen us as we journey toward your will of justice and peace.

All: **Amen.**

Serving the Food

Ritual words for Server

Server: We eat from one loaf. (bread)

We share one cup. (wine)

Songs during Distribution

"Give Us Today" (page 200) and other appropriate songs may be sung during distribution.

Postcommunion Litany (optional)

Leader: Jesus taught us these truths:
The world is filled with good things:

All: **may we all share in them equally.**

Leader: Sufficiency is the key to abundant life:

All: **help yourself and pass it along.**

Leader: Food is the gift of the Generous Spirit:

All: **thanks be to the Giver.**

Leader: We eat from one loaf:

All: **make room at the table.**

Postcommunion Prayer

Leader: Let us pray. Generous Spirit,

All: **thank you for this food. And thank you for the pleasures of eating together. With this meal you have given us both strength and hunger: strength for our bodies, strength for our community, and hunger for a world of justice. May we taste these same gifts at every meal. Amen.**

Postcommunion Song

"Now, O Spirit" (page 196).

BENEDICTION

Leader: Go now in joy and service —
        Scattering like tiny seeds.
        Trusting that you are in the right place.
        Rooting in the Soil of Infinite Love.
        Accepting the Invitation to emerge.
        Breaking up the pavement of greed and exclusion.
        And blooming in joyful bunches.

All: **We are the irrepressible weeds of peace. Amen.**

SENDING SONG

"Little by Little" (page 198), *or other appropriate song.*

PART THREE

RESOURCES FOR
TALKING, PRAYING, WORSHIPING

RESOURCE A

TALKING TOGETHER
ABOUT THIS BOOK
A GUIDE TO DISCUSSION

This book will be most valuable if it encourages ongoing conversations about the issues it raises. We hope that Part One will be used by congregations as a five-week study series and that Parts Two and Three will give worship leaders and congregations ideas and permission to try something different. We want people to try out some of our alternative suggestions, see how they feel, and continue their own journey to make worship and liturgy meaningful in today's world. We realize that each group will be in different places on the issues we raise and that many groups will be uncomfortable with some of the topics we broach and alternative suggestions we make. We offer this book in the spirit of open and honest dialog and as an invitation to address the difficult but important topics raised. Be honest. Be creative. Be welcoming. Be bold. Be humble. Have fun.

DISCUSSION QUESTIONS

The questions we provide at the end of the introduction and for chapters 1 through 4 are designed to encourage honest discussion, with an emphasis on probing personal feelings, reactions, and connections to issues raised. The questions fit within four categories that in our experience work well.[1] *Objective questions* get at content by probing core aspects of what the author is saying. *Reflective questions* get at participants' feelings and reactions to what is being said. *Interpretive questions* explore issues of meaning and why these issues are important or not important for individuals personally or for the church. *Decisional questions* encourage participants to probe their responses to the issues raised individually and collectively.

DISCUSSION LOGISTICS

This discussion approach is structured but open-ended. Objective questions can help get everyone on the same page and serve as a review of the chapter. Groups can then take the discussion wherever it needs to go without any predetermined outcome. *We recommend that groups include at least one question from each of the four categories.*

We suggest using a mix of small- and large-group discussion. If everything is done in a large group then only a small percentage of the group contributes, although everyone may have something important to say. A common process to use is the following:

- Ask participants to divide themselves into groups of three or four.

- Ask each group to spend a few minutes discussing the same question. Make sure each person has a chance to speak.

- Call the whole group back together and ask participants from the small groups to "popcorn" out phrases and highlights from their discussion.

- Re-form into small groups and repeat this process for each of the categories of questions.

We also suggest activities for each chapter. This is an alternative way to explore the material that embraces different learning styles. Activities can help spring the group into new ways of thinking. We encourage you to develop and use other activities involving art, music, role-plays, and skits. Feel free to take a risk and try something new.

Strong emotions like anger, fear, joy, resentment, or gratitude may arise as you discuss these chapters. Before you begin your discussion ask the group to create a set of two or three ground rules that will guide their time together. Such ground rules may include statements like: (1) we will share our true thoughts and feelings, (2) we will listen to each other with respect and an open heart, (3) we will take turns and encourage everyone to speak.

NOTES

1. R. Brian Stanfield, ed., *The Art of Focused Conversation: 100 Ways to Access Group Wisdom in the Workplace* (Philadelphia: New Society Publishers, 2000).

RESOURCE B

PRAYERS OF THE PEOPLE

I remember an interview with Mother Teresa in which she was asked what she said when she prayed. Her response was that she didn't say anything. She listened. She was then asked what God said when she listened. Her reply was that God doesn't say anything either. God just listens.

We'd like to encourage what might be a different form of prayer from what many groups are used to. Rather than a petitional form of prayer (asking for God's intervention through a list of petitions), we're hoping to establish a listening form of prayer, a time of mindfulness leading us into compassion. The former style of prayer (petitions) implies (to us) a god that is sometimes present, sometimes not, deciding who to hear, offering limited or conditional blessings. We prefer to be silent together, to become open; perhaps through the brief details of the real world we may hear the ever-present invitation.

In that spirit, we suggest that for prayers, allow a time when individuals simply lift up joys and concerns, naming them aloud:

- "John is in the hospital this week, in need of comfort and support."

- "The warblers have returned. I saw an indigo bunting yesterday."

- "Twenty-five thousand people died in an earthquake in Iran this week."

- "My mother and I spoke on the phone yesterday for the first time in three years."

Perhaps follow each with silence or a standardized couplet like one of the four that follow here:

Leader: Flower of Compassion:

All: Bloom in us.

—or—

Leader: Font of Mercy:

All: Well up in our hearts.

—or—

Leader: Love Unbounded:

All: We live in you.

—or—

Leader: God Who Is Mercy:

All: Receive our prayer.

RESOURCE C

PRAYERS TO PRINT AND READ TOGETHER

If you choose to have the group do a spoken prayer, the following incorporate some of the themes of this book.

1. PRAYER OF COMMITMENT[1]
(by Canaan Banana)

Open my eyes that they may see the deepest needs of my people.
Move my hands that they may feed the hungry.
Touch my heart that it may bring warmth to the despairing.
Teach me the generosity that welcomes strangers.
Let me share possessions to clothe the naked.
Give me the care that strengthens the sick.
Make me share in the quest to set the prisoners free.
In sharing our anxiety and our love,
our poverty and our prosperity,
we partake of your divine presence. Amen.

2. PRAYER FOR THE DECADE OF NONVIOLENCE[2]
(by Mary Lou Kownacki, OSB)

I bow to the sacred in all creation.

May my spirit fill the world with beauty and wonder.

May my mind seek truth with humility and openness.

May my heart forgive without limit.

May my love for friend, enemy, and outcast be without measure.

May my needs be few and my living simple.

May my actions bear witness to the suffering of others.

May my hands never harm a living being.

May my steps stay on the journey of justice.

May my tongue speak for those who are poor without fear of the powerful.

May my prayers rise with patient discontent until no child is hungry.

May my life's work be a passion for peace and nonviolence.

May my soul rejoice in the present moment.

May my imagination overcome death and despair with new possibility.

And may I risk reputation, comfort, and security to bring this hope to the children.

3. LORD'S PRAYER
(adap. Bret Hesla)

Gracious Spirit,
Who loves us like a mother,
Whose realm is blooming among us now. And within.
We pray that your compassion guide us in every action.
Give us what we need for each day,
and help us to be satisfied with the miracle of that alone.
Forgiver, whose embrace brings us to wholeness without our asking,
May we reconcile ourselves to one another in humility.
And may we cancel the crushing debts that imprison our neighbors
So that communities of joy and health may flourish.
May we neither profit from nor ignore evil.
But ever work to thwart it with nonviolence
As we co-create the realm of peace in this world.
Now and each day.
Amen.

NOTES

1. This prayer is by Canaan Banana from Zimbabwe. It is printed in *With All God's People: The New Ecumenical Prayer Cycle*, compiled by John Carden (Geneva: WCC Publications, 1989), 344.

2. This prayer is by Mary Lou Kownacki, OSB, and is used with permission from Pax Christi USA, www.paxchristiusa.org. It is distributed on a 3″ x 5″ card by Pax Christi USA, 532 W. 8th St., Erie, PA, 16502, to encourage prayer, study, and action to reduce violence. Cards can be ordered from Pax Christi ($10 per 100).

RESOURCES FOR GUIDING MEDITATION AND PRAYERS

Continuing with the theme of prayer as listening, we have used in many of the services a series of short readings and simple lists that can serve as guides to prayerful listening. These items (quotations, headlines, species names) can be read aloud and interspersed with silence and chant as a way to focus our prayer, to see the world as it truly is, and to hear the invitation into lives of richness and compassion. Below we sort these "lists" into three groups. (For a helpful guide to the use of readings, chant, and silence in worship, see the book *Prayer around the Cross* by Susan Briehl and Tom Witt.[1])

1. NEWSPAPER HEADLINES CALLING OUR ATTENTION TO THE WORLD AROUND US

The practice of using headlines as a guide for prayer has been around for quite a while. When these are read aloud, one at a time, and reflected on in silence, they can invite us into lives of compassion, to lives of service, to lives that engage the present moment and the world (see Service 2, "The Invitation," page 113). Depending on the focus of your prayer time, the headlines you gather could be limited to a particular theme (signs of hope, local concerns, international conflict, the natural world) or include a wide spectrum. Although your collection will undoubtedly reflect your biases to some extent, it's probably best to look for "factual reporting" headlines rather than opinion-page headlines.

STARTER LIST OF WORLD/NATIONAL POLITICAL HEADLINES

US Soldiers Ransack Sunni Mosque

Israel Jails Five as Dissent over Military Rises

US Begins Fingerprinting, Photographing Foreign Visitors

New Approach Needed for Sexual Predators

Somalis, Law Officers Work on Communication

Ramsey County's New Jail Already Nearing Capacity: Sheriff Beginning to Plan for Expansion

India, Pakistan Hold Peace Talks

British Soldiers "Kicked Iraqi Prisoner to Death"

A good online source for international news is www.commondreams.org.

STARTER LIST OF SOCIETY, PEOPLE HEADLINES

The Doors to Professions Widen: Women and Minorities Make Gains as Doctors and Lawyers

Ice Palace Show Produces the Irresistible Urge to Dance

Some Stores Are Saying No to Boy-Bashing Merchandise

Two Women Apply to Be Married: County Clerk Says Law Won't Allow It

Sounds of Silence: Educators Stress the Value of Uninterrupted Quiet Time

Project Helps Needy Buy Their Own Homes

Yelling at Kids Hurts Long Term, Study Says

Minneapolis Might Close Ten Schools: Jennings Blames Declining Enrollment, State Funding

These from newspapers, newsletters, neighborhood papers.

STARTER LIST OF ENVIRONMENTAL HEADLINES

Man Jailed for Damaging Yellowstone Area

Alaska Oil Exploration Approved

Airborne Ozone Can Alter Forest Soil

Study Shows Sea Ice at Poles Shrinking: Vanishing Ice May Destroy
Polar Bears' Habitat in 100 Years

Treated Wood Poses Cancer Risk to Kids

Genetic Alarm Clock Tells Plants When to Flower

Scientists Say Black Hole Stretched, Then Consumed a Star

2. SPECIES LISTS:
READINGS FROM THE "BOOK OF CREATION"

Our economy and our "prosperity" are heavily grounded in violence
against creation. Theologian Matthew Fox says our entire spirituality has
shriveled in part because we have neglected to include the cosmos in worship. We all need to be dreaming ways to restore that deficit. Perhaps the
thirteenth-century Christian mystic Meister Eckhart points us to one way
of doing this when he says, "All creation is a book about God, and every
creature is a word of God."[2] Why not use creation, and creatures, as the
readings during a service?

In the *Dawn of Creation* service (page 118) we invite you to read the
"word of God" together using lists of local flora and fauna. This reading
could proceed with five or six people reading aloud — simultaneously
and unplanned — from nonoverlapping lists. (For example, divide the list
below into six parts and find six readers.) Invite readers to take their time,
spreading the reading of their list over three minutes or so. (One thing
that happens for me as these names are read aloud is that I notice how
strange and unfamiliar the majority of them are to me. Then I get a little
feeling of loss and longing to be connected to all these near neighbors,
these wonders of creation.) State parks, local nature clubs, and field guides
are good sources for species lists. For example, here are a couple of lists
from around where we live.

BIRDS OF NORTHERN MINNESOTA

Lark Bunting
Savannah Sparrow
Le Conte's Sparrow
Fox Sparrow
Song Sparrow
Lincoln's Sparrow
Swamp Sparrow
White-throated Sparrow
Harris's Sparrow
White-crowned Sparrow
Dark-eyed Junco
Snow Bunting
Northern Cardinal
Rose-breasted Grosbeak
Indigo Bunting
Dickcissel
Bobolink
Red-winged Blackbird
Eastern Meadowlark
Western Meadowlark
Yellow-headed Blackbird
Rusty Blackbird
Brewer's Blackbird
Common Grackle
Brown-headed Cowbird
Baltimore Oriole
Pine Grosbeak
Purple Finch
Red Crossbill
White-winged Crossbill
Common Redpoll
Pine Siskin

American Goldfinch
Evening Grosbeak
House Sparrow
Gray Catbird
Brown Thrasher
European Starling
Bohemian Waxwing
Cedar Waxwing
Golden-winged Warbler
Tennessee Warbler
Orange-crowned Warbler
Nashville Warbler
Northern Parula
Yellow Warbler
Chestnut-sided Warbler
Magnolia Warbler
Cape May Warbler
Black-throated Blue Warbler
Yellow-rumped Warbler
Black-throated Green Warbler
Blackburnian Warbler
Pine Warbler
Palm Warbler
Bay-breasted Warbler
Blackpoll Warbler
Black-and-white Warbler
American Redstart
Prothonotary Warbler
Ovenbird
Northern Waterthrush
Connecticut Warbler
Mourning Warbler

Common Yellowthroat
Hooded Warbler
Wilson's Warbler
Canada Warbler
Scarlet Tanager
Eastern Towhee
American Tree Sparrow
Chipping Sparrow
Clay-colored Sparrow
Vesper Sparrow
Herring Gull
Caspian Tern
Common Tern
Forster's Tern
Black Tern
Rock Dove
Mourning Dove
Black-billed Cuckoo
Yellow-billed Cuckoo
Eastern Screech-Owl
Great Horned Owl
Snowy Owl
Barred Owl
Long-eared Owl
Short-eared Owl
Northern Saw-whet Owl
Common Nighthawk
Whip-poor-will
Chimney Swift
Magnificent Hummingbird
Ruby-throated Hummingbird
Belted Kingfisher
Red-headed Woodpecker
Williamson's Sapsucker
Yellow-bellied Sapsucker

Downy Woodpecker
Hairy Woodpecker
Three-toed Woodpecker
Black-backed Woodpecker
Northern Flicker
Pileated Woodpecker
Olive-sided Flycatcher
Eastern Wood Pewee
Yellow-bellied Flycatcher
Alder Flycatcher
Least Flycatcher
Eastern Phoebe
Great Crested Flycatcher
Western Kingbird
Cooper's Hawk
Northern Goshawk
Red-shouldered Hawk
Broad-winged Hawk
Red-tailed Hawk
Rough-legged Hawk
American Kestrel
Merlin
Peregrine Falcon
Ruffed Grouse
Spruce Grouse
Yellow Rail
Virginia Rail
Sora
American Coot
Sandhill Crane
Semipalmated Plover
Killdeer
Greater Yellowlegs
Lesser Yellowlegs
Solitary Sandpiper

Spotted Sandpiper

Upland Sandpiper

Marbled Godwit

Semipalmated Sandpiper

Least Sandpiper

White-rumped Sandpiper

Baird's Sandpiper

Pectoral Sandpiper

Dunlin

Stilt

Sandpiper

Short-billed Dowitcher

Common Snipe

American Woodcock

Wilson's Phalarope

Parasitic Jaeger

Franklin's Gull

Bonaparte's Gull

Ring-billed Gull

Common Loon

Pied-billed Grebe

Horned Grebe

Red-necked Grebe

Western Grebe

Double-crested Cormorant

Magnificent Frigatebird

American Bittern

Great Blue Heron

Great Egret

Cattle Egret

Green Heron

Black-crowned Night Heron

Turkey Vulture

Snow Goose

Canada Goose

Trumpeter Swan

Tundra Swan

Wood Duck

American Wigeon

American Black Duck

Mallard

Blue-winged Teal

Northern Shoveler

Green-winged Teal

Redhead

Ring-necked Duck

Lesser Scaup

Bufflehead

Common Goldeneye

Hooded Merganser

Common Merganser

Red-breasted Merganser

Ruddy Duck

Osprey

Swallow-tailed Kite

Bald Eagle

Northern Harrier

Sharp-shinned Hawk

COMMON WILDFLOWERS OF MINNESOTA

Water Plantain
Arrowhead
Duck-Potato
Wapato
Sweet Flag
Jack-in-the-Pulpit
Water Arum
Skunk Cabbage
Spiderwort
Cotton Grass
Wild Yam
Waterweed
Tapegrass
Eelgrass
Wild Celery
Blue Flag
Blue-eyed Grass
Wild Onion
Wild Leek
Bluebead Lily
Cory Lily
White Dog-tooth Violet
Trout Lily
Michigan Turk's-cap Lily
Wood Lily
False Lily of the Valley
Solomon's Seal
False Solomon's Seal
Carrion Flower
Twisted Stalk
False Asphodel
Nodding Trillium

Wake Robin
Declining Trillium
Large-flowered Trillium
Snow Trillium
Bellwort
Pale Bellwort
White Camass
Putty-Root
Dragon's Mouth
Swamp Pink
Grass Pink
Calypso
Spotted Coral Root
Stemless Lady Slipper
Moccasin Flower
Yellow Lady Slipper
Showy Lady Slipper
Tall White Orchid
Northern Green Orchid
Hooker's Orchid
Round-leafed Orchid
Ragged-fringed Orchid
Prairie White-fringed Orchid
Small Purple-fringed Orchid
Showy Orchid
Pickerel Weed
Bur-Reed
Narrow-leaved Cattail
Common Cattail
Floating-leaf Pondweed
Sago Pondweed
Flatstem Pondweed

Spreading Dogbane
Indian Hemp
Bristly Sarsaparilla
Wild Sarsaparilla
Spikenard
Ginseng
Wild Ginger
Swamp Milkweed
Showy Milkweed
Common Milkweed
Butterflyweed
Green Milkweed
Spotted Touch-me-not
Jewel Weed
Pale Touch-me-not
Blue Cohosh
May Apple
Mandrake
Hoary Puccoon
Narrow-leaved Puccoon
Tall Lungwort
Bluebell
Virginia Cowslip
False Gromwell
Prickly Pear Cactus
Tall Bellflower
Harebell
Cardinal Flower
Great Lobelia
Sandwort
Field Chickweed
Common Mouse-ear Chickweed
White Campion
Smooth Catchfly
Long-leaved Chickweed

Common Chickweed
Yarrow
Milfoil
False Dandelion
Pearly Everlasting
Ladies Tobacco
Dogfennel
Chamomile
Western Mugwort
White Sage
Lindley's Aster
Frost-weed Aster
Smooth Aster
Large-leaved Aster
New England Aster
Beggar-Ticks
Great Indian Plantain
Tuberous Indian Plantain
Chicory
Ox-eye Daisy
Golden Aster
Hill's Thistle
Swamp Thistle
Tickseed
Coneflower
Purple Coneflower
Philadelphia Fleabane
Joe-pye Weed
White Snakeroot
Low Cudweed
Gumweed
Sneezeweed
Common Sunflower
Blue Lettuce
Blazing Star

Rattlesnake Root
Prairie Coneflower
Goldenglow
Black-eyed Susan
Golden Ragwort
Prairie Ragwort
Compass Plant
Cup-plant
Tall Goldenrod
Zig-Zag Goldenrod
Grass-leaved Goldenrod
Stiff Goldenrod
Goat's Beard
Western Ironweed
Field Bindweed
Wild Morning Glory
Pink Rock Cress
Tower Mustard
Common Winter Cress
Yellow Rocket
Hoary Alyssum
Charlock
Spring Cress
Toothwort
Draba
Western Wallflower
Water Cress
Wild Cucumber
Bur Cucumber
Oblong-leaved Sundew
Flowering Spurge
Cypress Spurge
Leafy Spurge
Dutchman's Breeches
St. John's Wort

Prairie Gentian
Wild Geranium
Virginia Waterleaf
Fragrant Giant Hyssop
Ground Ivy
Motherwort
Wild Bergamot
Catnip
Common Skullcap
Small Skullcap
Hog Peanut
Canadian Milk Vetch
Prairie Plum
White False Indigo
Wild Pea
Wild Lupine
Locoweed
Indian Breadroot
White Clover
American Vetch
Bladderwort
Purple Loosestrife
Common Mallow
Wild Four-o-clock
Yellow Water Lily
Fireweed
Evening Primrose
Wood Sorrel
Sheep Sorrel
Bloodroot
Plantain
Wild Blue Phlox
Jacob's Ladder
Seneca Snakeroot
Yellow Dock

3. SHORT QUOTATIONS TO READ ALOUD AND ALTERNATE WITH CHANT AND SILENCE

Several of the services use short readings to support prayerful meditation. We are reprinting these shorter quotations here so that you have them all in one place, along with a source. We hope this collection will:

- help you select the ones you may want to use to focus your group's prayer and meditation

- remind you of similar important favorites of yours to collect and use.

◆

Those who say religion has nothing to do with politics do not know what religion means. — MAHATMA GANDHI[3]

◆

Unrolling the scroll, Jesus found the place where it is written: God has anointed me to preach the good news to the poor, to proclaim release to the captives and recovering of sight to the blind; to set at liberty those who are oppressed, to proclaim the acceptable year of Yahweh.

— LUKE 4:17–19, PARAPHRASE

◆

What good is it to me if Mary gave birth to Jesus 1400 years ago if I do not also give birth to him in my time and my culture?

— MEISTER ECKHART, THIRTEENTH CENTURY[4]

◆

But a Samaritan on the road was moved with compassion when he saw this victim. He went up to him and bandaged his wounds, pouring oil and wine on them. Then he lifted him up to his own donkey, carried him to the inn, and looked after him. . . . Go and do the same yourself.

— JESUS, FROM LUKE 10:33–35,37, PARAPHRASE

◆

In the face of suffering, one has no right to turn away.... In the face of injustice, one may not look the other way.... To watch over a [person] that grieves is a more urgent duty than to think of God.

— ELIE WIESEL, NOBEL LAUREATE AND HOLOCAUST SURVIVOR[5]

◆

I stressed the need for a social gospel to supplement the gospel of individual salvation. I suggested that only a "dry as dust" religion prompts a minister to extol the glories of heaven while ignoring the social conditions that cause people an earthly hell.... I asked how *our people* would ever gain *their* freedom without the guidance, support, and inspiration of *their* spiritual leaders.   — MARTIN LUTHER KING JR., ABOUT SPEAKING TO
A GROUP OF MINISTERS, PARAPHRASE[6]

◆

How filled with awe is this place, and we did not know it.

— GATES OF PRAYER[7]

◆

Glance at the sun. See the moon and the stars.
Gaze at the beauty of earth's greenings. Now, think.
What delight God gives to humankind with all these things.

— HILDEGARD OF BINGEN, TWELFTH CENTURY[8]

◆

The word goes forth from the mouth of God, and does not return empty.

— ISAIAH 55, PARAPHRASE

◆

Notice how the wild lilies grow: They don't slave and they never spin. Yet let me tell you, even Solomon at the height of his glory was never decked out like one of these.   — JESUS, IN MATTHEW 6:28–29, PARAPHRASE

◆

Every creature is a word of God, and all creation is a book about God.

— MEISTER ECKHART, THIRTEENTH CENTURY[9]

What is the test that you have indeed undergone this holy birth?
Listen carefully. If this birth has truly taken place within you,
then every single creature points you toward God.

— MEISTER ECKHART, THIRTEENTH CENTURY[10]

God is creating the entire universe
fully and totally in this present now.
Everything God created in the beginning —
and even previous to that . . .
God creates now all at once.

— MEISTER ECKHART, THIRTEENTH CENTURY[11]

The days pass and the years vanish,
and we walk sightless among miracles.
Creator, fill our eyes with seeing and our minds with knowing;
Let there be moments when the candles of your Presence
illumine the darkness in which we walk.

— ADAPTED FROM GATES OF PRAYER[12]

With what can we compare God's realm, or what parable will we use for it? It is like a mustard seed, which, when sown upon the ground, is the smallest of all the seeds on earth; yet when it is sown it grows up and becomes the greatest of shrubs, and puts forth large branches, so that the birds can make nests in its shade.

— JESUS, IN MARK 4:30–32, PARAPHRASE

The mustard plant is dangerous even when domesticated in the garden, and it is deadly when growing wild in the grain fields. And those nesting birds, which may strike us as charming, represented to ancient farmers a permanent danger to the seed and the grain. The point, in other words, is not just that the mustard plant starts as a proverbially small seed and grows into a shrub of three, four, or even more feet in height. It is that it tends to take over where it is not wanted, that it tends to get out of control, and that it tends to attract birds within cultivated areas, where they are not particularly desired. And that, says Jesus, was what the Kingdom was like. Like a pungent shrub with dangerous take-over properties.

— JOHN DOMINIC CROSSAN, CONCERNING THE IMAGE
OF THE MUSTARD SEED[13]

◆

The realm of God "is already breaking into the world, and it comes, not as an imposition from on high, but as the leaven slowly causing the dough to rise."   — WALTER WINK[14]

◆

The time is always ripe to do right. Now is the time to make real the promise of democracy and transform our pending national elegy into a creative psalm of *humanity*. Now is the time to lift our national policy from the quicksand of racial injustice to the solid rock of human dignity.

— MARTIN LUTHER KING JR., PARAPHRASE[15]

◆

Friend, hope for the Guest while you are alive.
Jump into experience while you are alive!
Think . . . and think . . . while you are alive.
What you call "salvation" belongs to the time before death.
If you don't break your ropes while you are alive,
Do you think
Ghosts will do it after?
The idea that the soul will join with the ecstatic
Just because the body is rotten —

That is all fantasy.
What is found now is found then.
If you find nothing now,
You will simply end up with an apartment in the city of Death.
If you make love with the divine now, in the next life
You will have the face of satisfied desire.

— KABIR, FIFTEENTH CENTURY, INDIA[16]

The time has come.
The realm of God is near.   — JESUS, IN MARK 1:15, PARAPHRASE

In music, in the sea, in a flower, in a leaf, in an act of kindness.
... I see what people call God in all these things.

— PABLO CASALS, MUSICIAN[17]

Nobody sees a flower, really. It is so small, it takes time — we haven't
time. And to see takes time, like to have a friend takes time.

— GEORGIA O'KEEFFE, AMERICAN PAINTER[18]

Whatever God does, the first outburst is always compassion.

— MEISTER ECKHART, THIRTEENTH CENTURY[19]

Be you compassionate, as your Creator is compassionate.

— JESUS, IN LUKE 6:36, PARAPHRASE

There was a man going from Jerusalem down to Jericho when he fell into
the hands of robbers. They stripped him, beat him up, and left him half
dead by the roadside. Now by coincidence a priest was going down that
road; when he caught sight of the man, he went out of his way to avoid

him. In the same way, when a Levite came to the place, he took one look at the man and crossed the road to avoid him. But this Samaritan who was traveling that way came to where the man was and was moved to pity at the sight of him. He went up to him and bandaged his wounds, pouring olive oil and wine on them. He hoisted him onto his own animal, brought him to an inn, and looked after him.... Go and do likewise.

— JESUS, IN LUKE 10:30–34, 37, PARAPHRASE

◆

Every act of love is a work of peace, no matter how small. The fruit of love is service. The fruit of service is peace.   — MOTHER TERESA[20]

◆

God is love.   — I JOHN 4:8

◆

When I can no longer bear my loneliness, I take it to my friends. For I must share it with all the friends of God. "Do you suffer?" "So do I!"

— MECHTILD OF MAGDEBURG, THIRTEENTH CENTURY[21]

◆

Joy was in fact the most characteristic result of all Jesus' activity amongst the poor and the oppressed.   — ALBERT NOLAN[22]

◆

I am human. Nothing human is alien to me.

— ROMAN PLAYWRIGHT TERENCE, SECOND CENTURY B.C.E.

◆

Air, blowing everywhere, serves all creatures.

— HILDEGARD OF BINGEN, TWELFTH CENTURY[23]

◆

You have heard that it was said, "You shall love your neighbor and hate your enemy." But I say to you, love your enemies and pray for those who persecute you, so that you may be children of God, for God makes the sun rise on the evil and on the good, and sends rain on the righteous and on the unrighteous.   — JESUS, IN MATT 5:43–45, PARAPHRASE.

I'm not into isms and asms. There isn't a Catholic moon and a Baptist sun. I know the universal God is universal.... I feel that the same God-force that is the mother and father of the pope is the mother and father of the loneliest wino on the planet.   — DICK GREGORY[24]

Once Jesus was asked by the Pharisees when God's realm was coming, and he answered, "It is not coming with things that can be observed; nor will they say, 'Look, here it is!' or 'There it is!' For in fact, it is already among you."   — FROM LUKE 17:20–21, PARAPHRASE

When we are mindful, touching deeply the present moment, we can see and listen deeply, and the fruits are always understanding, acceptance, love, and the desire to relieve suffering and bring joy.

— THICH NHAT HANH[25]

NOTES

1. Susan Briehl and Tom Witt, *Prayer around the Cross: A Guide to the Liturgy* (Chelan, Wash.: Holden Village Press, 1999). Available at www.holdenvillage.org/bookstore/hvpress.html.

2. Quoted in Matthew Fox, *Original Blessing: A Primer in Creation Spirituality* (Santa Fe, N.Mex.: Bear and Company, 1983).

3. Mohandas K. Gandhi, *An Autobiography: The Story of My Experiments with the Truth*, trans. M. Desai (Boston: Beacon Press, 1968), 504.

4. In Fox, *Original Blessing*, 221.

5. Harry James Cargas, *Harry James Cargas in Conversation with Elie Wiesel* (New York: Paulist Press, 1976), 3.

6. Martin Luther King Jr., *Why We Can't Wait* (New York: HarperCollins, 1964), 67.

7. Excerpted from *Gates of Prayer: The New Union Prayer Book* (New York: Central Conference of American Rabbis, 1975). Used by permission.

8. In Fox, *Original Blessing*, 68.

9. In ibid., 35.

10. In ibid., 108.

11. In ibid., 68.

12. Excerpted from *Gates of Prayer: The New Union Prayer Book* (New York: Central Conference of American Rabbis, 1975). Used by permission.

13. John Dominic Crossan, *Jesus: A Revolutionary Biography* (New York: HarperCollins, 1995), 65.

14. Walter Wink, *Engaging the Powers: Discernment and Resistance in a World of Domination* (Minneapolis: Fortress Press, 1992).

15. King, *Why We Can't Wait*, 86.

16. Robert Bly, *The Kabir Book*, 103. Copyright © 1971, 1977 by Robert Bly; © 1977 by the Seventies Press. Reprinted by permission of Beacon Press, Boston.

17. Cited in David Blum, *Casals and the Art of Interpretation* (Berkeley: University of California Press, 1980), 208.

18. Cited in Julia Cameron, *The Artist's Way* (New York: G. P. Putnam's Sons, 1992), 22.

19. In Fox, *Original Blessing*, 277.

20. Mother Teresa, *A Simple Path*, compiled by Lucinda Vardey (New York: Ballantine Books, 1995).

21. In Fox, *Original Blessing*, 145.

22. Albert Nolan, *Jesus before Christianity* (Maryknoll, N.Y.: Orbis Books, 1978), 41.

23. In Fox, *Original Blessing*, 277.

24. In ibid., 67.

25. Thich Nhat Hanh, *Living Buddha, Living Christ* (New York: Riverhead Books, 1995).

COMMITMENT STATEMENTS

Commitment statements help us to express our unity, not in terms of our doctrine, but in terms of our lifestyle — both as individuals and as a community. The best "Commitment Statement" would be one your group would hash out together in response to the question, "What is important to us in how we live out our faith in this world?" It may be helpful to try to focus the discussion on "how we strive to live" as opposed to "what we believe about God." As some issues and patterns begin to emerge, write them down and sort them into categories for all to see: "Points of emerging agreement," "Points of disagreement," and "Need further discussion." Using the first of these lists, try to arrive at three or four short sentences that can work as a group statement, perhaps beginning with a sentence like, "We are united in our belief that our faith calls us to act justly in the world and so we are a community seeking what it means to follow the invitation of Jesus to abundant life...." Let the statement grow and change with your ongoing dialog.

Below are a few statements that might serve as models, or jumping-off points for dialog.

1. DECALOGUE OF ASSISI FOR PEACE

Issued by participants of many world religions who attended the worldwide Day of Prayer for Peace, January 24, 2002, convened by the Vatican.[1]

1. We commit ourselves to proclaiming our firm conviction that violence and terrorism are incompatible with the authentic spirit of religion, and as we condemn every recourse to violence and war in the name of god or of religion, we commit ourselves to doing everything possible to eliminate the root causes of terrorism.

2. We commit ourselves to educating people to mutual respect and esteem....

3. We commit ourselves to fostering the culture of dialog....

4. We commit ourselves to defending the right of everyone to live a decent life....

5. We commit ourselves to frank and patient dialog, refusing to consider our differences as an insurmountable barrier.

6. We commit ourselves to forgiving one another for past and present errors and prejudices, and to supporting one another in a common effort both to overcome selfishness and arrogance, hatred and violence, and to learn from the past that peace without justice is no true peace.

7. We commit ourselves to taking the side of the poor and helpless....

8. We commit ourselves to taking up the cry of those who refuse to be resigned to violence and evil....

9. We commit ourselves to encouraging all efforts to promote friendship between peoples, for we are convinced that, in the absence of solidarity and understanding between peoples, technological progress exposes the world to a growing risk of destruction and death.

10. We commit ourselves to urging leaders of nations to make every effort to create and consolidate, on the national and international levels, a world of solidarity and peace based on justice.

2. PRECEPTS FOR LIVING

From the Buddhist peacemaker Thich Nhat Hanh[2]

1. Do not be idolatrous about or bound to any doctrine, theory, or ideology.

2. Do not think that the knowledge you presently possess is changeless, absolute truth.

3. Do not force others, including children, by any means whatsoever, to adopt your views, whether by authority, threat, money, propaganda, or even education.

4. Do not avoid contact with suffering or close your eyes before suffering.

5. Do not accumulate wealth while millions are hungry.... Possess nothing that should belong to others.

6. Do not maintain anger or hatred.

7. Do not lose yourself in dispersion and in your surroundings. Learn to practice mindfulness.

8. Do not utter words that can create discord and cause the community to break.

9. Do not say untruthful things for the sake of personal interest or to impress people.

10. Do not live with a vocation that is harmful to humans and nature.

11. Do not kill. Do not let others kill.

12. Do not mistreat your body.

3. COMMITMENT TO LEARNING THE WAYS OF JESUS

By Bret Hesla

We are united in believing that our faith calls us to act justly in the world and so we are a community committed to learning: learning what it means to follow the invitation of Jesus to abundant life.

- We are learning to ignore the noisy graffiti of scarcity and fear.
- We are learning to see sufficiency as the end, not the beginning.
- We are learning to give thanks for all that we have and to share it with whoever needs it.
- We are learning each to contribute what we can, aware of our place in the world.

- We are learning to uplift the many who are left out of the earth's uneven abundance.

- We are learning to undo the hoarding of those with wrongful power and privilege.

- We are learning to resist militarism and its corrupting of our national culture.

- We are learning to find joy in savoring rather than consuming.

- We will support one another in mutual prayer and dialog as we individually and collectively try to learn these ways.

4. OTHER RESOURCES: UN DECADE OF NONVIOLENCE

The United Nations, along with a wide spectrum of world religions and Nobel laureates, has declared 2000–2010 the Decade of Nonviolence. There are many documents and responses to this declaration, resources and action guides from which congregations could craft some commitment statements. Here are a few places to start.

www.forusa.org/programs/decade.html

www.elca.org/co/decade.html

www3.unesco.org

Much of the language in the original UN document urges nations and organizations to work toward establishing a "culture of peace."

NOTES

1. Online at www.Vatican.va/special/Assisi_20020124_en.html
2. Thich Nhat Hanh, *Being Peace* (Berkeley: Parallax Press, 1987), 89–100.

READINGS

READING 1:
"ANYWAY," BY MOTHER TERESA[1]

People are unreasonable, illogical, and self-centered.
> Love them anyway.
If you do good, people may accuse you of selfish motives.
> Do good anyway.
If you are successful, you may win false friends and true enemies.
> Succeed anyway.
The good you do today may be forgotten tomorrow.
> Do good anyway.
Honesty and transparency make you vulnerable.
> Be honest and transparent anyway.
What you spend years building may be destroyed overnight.
> Build anyway.
People who really want help may attack you if you help them.
> Help them anyway.
Give the world the best you have and you may get hurt.
> Give the world your best anyway.

READING 2:
FROM BARBARA KINGSOLVER[2]

Hallie is writing to her sister Codi. She writes from Nicaragua, under a U.S.-led attack. Hallie writes this about hope:

You're thinking of revolution as a great all-or-nothing. I think of it as one more morning in a muggy cotton field, checking the undersides of leaves to see what's been there, figuring out what to do that won't clear a path for worse problems next week. Right now that's what I do. You ask why I'm not afraid of loving and losing, and that's my answer. Wars and elections are both too big and too small to matter in the long run. The daily work — that goes on, it adds up. It goes into the ground, into crops, into children's bellies and their bright eyes. Good things don't get lost.

Codi, here's what I've decided: the very least you can do in your life is to figure out what you hope for. And the most you can do is live inside that hope. Not admire it from a distance but live right in it, under its roof. What I want is so simple I almost can't say it: elementary kindness. Enough to eat, enough to go around. The possibility that kids might one day grow up to be neither the destroyers nor the destroyed. That's about it. Right now I'm living in that hope, running down its hallway and touching the walls on both sides. I can't tell you how good it feels. I wish you knew.

READING 3:
FROM MADELEINE DELBREL[3]

We, the ordinary people of the streets, believe with all our might that this street, this world, where God has placed us, is our place of holiness.

We find that prayer is action and that action is prayer. It seems to us that truly loving action is filled with light. . . . Our feet march upon a street, but our heartbeat reverberates through the whole world. That is why our small acts, which we can't decide whether they're action or contemplation, perfectly join together the love of God and the love of our neighbor. . . . Each docile act makes us receive God totally and give God totally, in a great freedom of spirit. And thus life becomes a celebration. Each tiny act is an extraordinary event, in which heaven is given to us, in which we are able to give heaven to others. It makes no difference what we do, whether we take in hand a broom or a pen. Whether we speak or keep silent. Whether we are sewing or holding a meeting, caring for a sick person or tapping away at a typewriter. Whatever it is, it's just the outer shell of an amazing inner reality: the soul's encounter, renewed at each moment, in which, at each moment, the soul grows in grace and becomes ever more beautiful for her God. Is the doorbell ringing? Quick, open the door! It's God coming to love us. Is someone asking us to do something? Here you are! . . . it's God coming to love us.

READING 4:
FROM THICH NHAT HANH

When there are wars within us, it will not be long before we are at war with others, even those we love. The violence, hatred, discrimination, and fear in society water the seeds of the violence, hatred, discrimination, and fear in us. If we go back to ourselves and to touch our feelings, we will see the ways that we furnish fuel for the wars going on inside. Meditation is, first of all, a tool for surveying our own territory so we can know what is going on. With the energy of mindfulness, we can calm things down, understand them, and bring harmony back to the conflicting elements inside us. If we can learn ways to touch the peace, joy, and happiness that are already there, we will become healthy and strong, and a resource for others.[4]

In Buddhism, our effort is to practice mindfulness in each moment — to know what is going on within and all around us. . . . Most of the time, we are lost in the past or carried away by future projects and concerns. When we are mindful, touching deeply the present moment, we can see and listen deeply, and the fruits are always understanding, acceptance, love, and the desire to relieve suffering and bring joy. . . . To me, mindfulness is very much like the Holy Spirit. Both are agents of healing. When you have mindfulness, you have love and understanding, you see more deeply, and you can heal the wounds in your own mind.[5]

We often think of peace as the absence of war, that if the powerful countries would reduce their weapons arsenals, we could have peace. But if we look deeply into the weapons, we see our own minds — our prejudices, fears, and ignorance. Even if we transport all the bombs to the moon, the roots of war and the roots of the bombs are still here, in our hearts and minds, and sooner or later we will make new bombs. To work for peace is to uproot war from ourselves and from the hearts of men and women.

To prepare for war, to give millions of men and women the opportunity to practice killing day and night in their hearts, is to plant millions of seeds of violence, anger, frustration, and fear that will be passed on for generations to come.... There must be ways to solve our conflicts without killing. We must look at this. We have to find ways to help people get out of difficult situations, situations of conflict, without having to kill. Our collective wisdom and experience can be the torch lighting *our path, showing us what to do. Looking deeply together is the main task of a community or a church.* (Emphasis in original)[6]

READING 5:
THE SHAKERTOWN PLEDGE[7]

Recognizing that the earth and the fullness thereof is a gift from our gracious God, and that we are called to cherish, nurture, and provide loving stewardship for the earth's resources;

And recognizing that life itself is a gift, and a call to responsibility, joy, and celebration;

I make the following declarations:

1. I declare myself to be a world citizen.

2. I commit myself to lead an ecologically sound life.

3. I commit myself to lead a life of creative simplicity and to share my personal wealth with the world's poor.

4. I commit myself to join with others in reshaping institutions in order to bring about a more just global society in which each person has full access to the needed resources for their physical, emotional, intellectual, and spiritual growth.

5. I commit myself to occupational accountability, and in so doing, I will seek to avoid the creation of products which cause harm to others.

6. I affirm the gift of my body, and commit myself to its proper nourishment and physical well-being.

7. I commit myself to examine continually my relations with others, and to attempt to relate honestly, morally, and lovingly to those around me.

8. I commit myself to personal renewal through prayer, meditation, and study.

9. I commit myself to responsible participation in a community of faith.

NOTES

1. Mother Teresa, *Meditations from a Simple Path,* cited in Colman McCarthy, ed., *Strength through Peace: The Ideas and People of Nonviolence* (Washington, D.C.: Center for Teaching Peace), 77.

2. The quote is from Barbara Kingsolver, *Animal Dreams* (New York: HarperCollins, 1990), 299.

3. Madeleine Delbrêl, *We the Ordinary People of the Streets,* English trans. (Grand Rapids, Mich.: Wm. B. Eerdmans, 2000), 54, 57–58. Delbrêl, who lived from 1904 to 1964, founded a core group of professional women that worked for thirty years among French communists, working people, immigrants, and the poor. She advanced a practical spirituality combined with a contemplative approach to ordinary life.

4. Thich Nhat Hanh, *Living Buddha, Living Christ* (New York: Riverhead Books, 1995), 19.

5. Ibid., 14.

6. Ibid., 76–77.

7. From *Taking Charge* by the Simple Living Collective and American Friends Service Committee (1977), one of the precursors to the Voluntary Simplicity movement. Available at http://underground.musenet.org:8080/orenda/shakertown.txt.

USING THESE SERVICES
THE POLITICS OF DOING SOMETHING NEW

1. INTRODUCING THESE SERVICES
TO YOUR CONGREGATION

The services in Part Two include all sorts of new elements — songs, prayers, meditation. Even "communion" is quite different. Does that mean these services are only for the small ghetto of the "Christian left"? We hope not. For sure, doing this much new material all at once will be a challenge to most congregations and worshiping groups. We think you should just "go for it." But if you want to ease into it a little, here are a couple of ways to get used to the water before you all jump in.

- Invite people to be involved in planning and leading. Include lots of folks in preplanning, strategizing, teaching music, and then leading parts. There are many opportunities for readers — in some services you could use five or six different readers.

- Ask for help. People want to help, to make things work. If you ask for help, people are "onboard" from the start.

- Invite a member of the congregation (or schedule an adult forum) to write or adapt one of the litanies.

- Begin learning the music one song at a time, as part of your other services, so that when you put it all together, it has gained some familiarity.

- Teach the choir the music, so they can provide a strong core of voices for the new material.

- Find a confident song leader (not a trained soloist) who can stand up front and lead folks through the music.

- Establish a ten-minute singing time before each service to go through the songs in advance.

- Insert a familiar song here or there, especially toward the beginning.

- Start with a time slot other than Sunday morning. Try a six-week series of evening services, perhaps sponsored by your social action committee.

- Remember that in music and worship, familiarity breeds comfort. Plan to do a service many times. Perhaps introduce it as a six-week series, giving it some time to become familiar. Then repeat it the following year during the same six-week period. Over time it becomes a comfortable routine and develops meaning through seasonal repetition.

2. INVITE DISCUSSION AFTER INTRODUCING A NEW SERVICE

Schedule a structured feedback time after you first introduce a new worship service. You may even want to bill the event as a "new worship service and a follow-up discussion." Since people want to give their responses to new worship ideas, do it as a group. This process empowers a congregation and avoids the feelings of "When are they going to pull another one on us?" Using the following discussion questions, invite folks to talk about the service: What worked? What didn't? What felt good? What felt strange? When shall we try it again? Ask one or more of the questions in each of the following categories.

Objective Questions

- What stands out for you about this service?
- What parts do you remember?

Reflective Questions

- How did you feel during the service?
- Were there any parts of the service you really liked?

- Were there any parts of the service that disturbed you? Or you thought were just weird?

Interpretive Questions

- What was different about this service from "what we usually do"?
- What kinds of "meaning" were in this service that are missing from our usual service?
- What kinds of "meaning" were missing from this service that our other services have?

Decisional Questions

- How would doing a service like this regularly affect our congregation?
- Does this give us any ideas about how to expand what we do in worship?
- How could we make it better when we do this service again?
- Now what should we do?

RESOURCE H

SONGS

We Gather Longing

With an easy lilt (swing 8ths)

1. We gath-er long-ing, long-ing for peace.
2. We gath-er sing-ing joy-ful-ly strong.
3. We gath-er dream-ing what is to be.
4. We gath-er pray-ing the heart of the world.

We gath-er long-ing, long-ing for peace.
We gath-er sing-ing joy-ful-ly strong.
We gath-er dream-ing what is to be.
We gath-er pray-ing the heart of the world.

We gath-er long-ing, long-ing for peace, and we know
We gath-er sing-ing joy-ful-ly strong, and we know
We gath-er dream-ing what is to be, and we know
We gath-er pray-ing the heart of the world, and we know

it's good to be here.
it's good to be here.
it's good to be here.
it's good to be here.

Words and music © 2004 Bret Hesla

(Optional refrain to follow any verse:)

We are long - ing,* long - ing,

long - ing, long - ing for peace. We are long - ing,

long - ing, long - ing, long - ing for peace.

* or "singing", "praying", etc. -- adapt refrain accordingly.

Here In This Ordinary Place

Lively

1. May we a-wake, a-wak-en to the pre-sence of God,
2. May we a-wake a-wak-en to the pow-er of love,
3. And may we build a neigh-bor-hood of jus-tice for all,
4. And may we dai-ly work to build a world___ at peace.

pre-sence of God, the pre-sence of God. May we a-
pow-er of love, the pow-er of love. May we a-
jus-tice for all, jus-tice for all. And may we
world___ at peace, a world___ at peace. And may we

Call* : Here in this place

wake, a-wak-en to the pre-sence of God
wake a-wak-en to the pow-er of love
build a neigh-bor-hood of jus-tice for all
dai-ly work to build a world___ at peace.

1. *May we awake....*
2. *Here in this place...*

here in this or-din-ar-y place.
here in this or-din-ar-y crowd.
now in this or-din-ar-y time.
now with these or-din-ar-y hands.

place.
crowd.
time.
hands.

* See CD-ROM for the call part, indicated here in text only

Words and music © 1999 Bret Hesla

Here in this place.   *Here in this place.*

Here._____ Here in this or - din - ar - y place.
Here,_____ here in this or - din - ar - y crowd.
Now,_____ now in this or - din - ar - y time.
Now,_____ now with these or - din - ar - y hands.

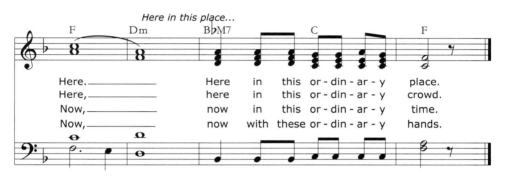

Here in this place...

Here._____ Here in this or - din - ar - y place.
Here,_____ here in this or - din - ar - y crowd.
Now,_____ now in this or - din - ar - y time.
Now,_____ now with these or - din - ar - y hands.

Flower of Compassion (#1)

Words and music © 2004 Bret Hesla

Optional accompaniment while prayer is spoken between verses 1 and 2.

(Leader: We pray for a bond of love.....)

Optional accompaniment while prayer is spoken between verses 2 and 3.

(Leader: We pray for a culture of peace....)

Come Lend Your Beauty to This Place

Dancing merrily

1. Mine is the church where ev'-ry-bo-dy's wel-come. I know it's true, 'cause I got through the door. We are a dazz-ling bou-quet of ev-ery
2. Come gath-er round, you six-foot glad-i-o-las. Come all you pur-ple li-lacs shin-ing bright. Come let us all bloom to-geth-er in one
3. Don't think we mere-ly tol-er-ate each oth-er. We ask and tell, we don't just turn a-way. We give at-ten-tion to ev-ery bud and
4. We see our de-mons try-ing to di-vide us; They doc-u-ment their lies to make them true. To-day we're freed from our judg-ing and ex-

flow - er. Jump in the vase, 'cause we've got space for more.
gar - den: A car - ni - val of fra-grance and de - light.
blos-som. Let ev - ery face come grace the grand bou - quet.
clu - ding. Just look a - round en - joy this love-ly view.

Refrain: We are a daz - zling bou - quet, a daz - zling bou - quet, a

daz-zling bou-quet of ev-ery flow-er. We are a daz-zling bou-quet, a

daz - zling bou - quet. Come, lend your beau-ty to this place.

191

Make Us Mindful

Note: Choose one verse and use it throughout, as described
in the service "Here In This Ordinary Place."

Heart of Mercy

The Open Invitation

1. Sound the call of wel-come. Ev'-ry-one come.
2. The door is al-ways o-pen.
3. We're or - din-ar - y peo-ple.

Sound the call of wel - come. Ev' - ry - one come. Oh, sound
Door is al - ways o - pen. The ta -
Or - din - ar - y bod - ies. An or -

the call of wel - come. Ev' - ry - one come. The O -
ble's set and wait - ing.
din - ar - y pot - luck.

pen In - vi - ta - tion stands. *(to bridge after verses 3 & 6)*

Words and music ©1999 Bret Hesla

Bridge: Grate-ful we stand at the ta-ble of peace:

Spir-it of Mer-cy re-vealed.

Wo-ven to-geth-er, weal-thy and poor,

through one a-noth-er we're healed. *(to next verse)*

4. It's not a victory party.....
It's not for members only....
No matter what your creed is.....

5. It's time to tell our stories....
To listen to each other....
Be shoulder next to shoulder....

6. Without any condition....
Without any coercion...
Without any exception....*(to Bridge)*

7. The Spirit is among us....
The Spirit is within us.....
The Spirit is inviting....

195

Now, O Spirit

With gusto

1. Now, O Spir - it, fill us with fire. Your com - pas - sion be our de - sire. Now, O Spir - it, o - pen our hands. May we share as need___ de - mands. Let - ting go of what is not ours, True a - bun - dance ev - 'ry - where flowers.

2. Now, O Spir - it, giv - er of breath Free us from con - su - ming death. May we throt - tle run - a - way "More," mon - key wrench the gears___ of war. Meet op - pres - sion face___ to face We re - sist in non - vi - o - lent ways.

3. Now, O Spir - it, turn us a - side In our qui - et mo - ments con - fide. Heal - ing Womb, En - vel - o - ping Urn We in you de - vel - op and learn. In the night, your si - lence we hear. By your calm___ we cer - tain - ly steer.

4. Pour - ing Spir - it, Swig of De - light Cup of Joy, all peo - ple u - nite. Shine, O Sweet Ex - pres - sion of Grace. Be re - vealed in ev - 'ry face. Shar - ing food our spir - its we blend; Truths dis - cov - ered in stran - ger and friend.

Words and music © 2003 Bret Hesla

196

Dai - ly giv - ing jus - tice birth: Dawn___ of peace,

a la - bor - ing earth.

Little By Little

With joyful resolve (swing 8ths)

Verses (melody same as chorus):

1. Growing in cracks and crevices (3x), we are everywhere.
2. Habits of peace and justice (3x): tools to change the world. (Ch.)

3. Never resorting to violence (3x), we will find a way.
4. Working with all of each other (3x), we are not alone. (Ch.)

5. The Spirit is present among us (3x), we are filled with power.
6. Rooted in the Water of Mercy (3x), we will surely flower. (Ch.)

Words and music © 2003 Bret Hesla

Give Us Our Daily Bread

Prayerfully, tenderly

1. Give us our dai - ly bread. Give us our dai - ly bread.
2. May we be sa - tis - fied. May we be sa - tis - fied.
3. Nev - er be sa - tis - fied. Nev - er be sa - tis - fied.
4. Pass - ing the gift a - long. Pass - ing the gift a - long.

Give us our dai - ly bread.
May we be sa - tis - fied.
Nev - er be sa - tis - fied.
Pass - ing the gift a - long.

May we be sa - tis - fied.
With on - ly what we need.
If an - y be de - nied.
Each add - ing as we can.

5. Five thou-sand will be fed.
Five thou-sand will be fed.
Five thou-sand will be fed.
Trust-ing there be e-nough.

Give Us Today

With spirit

Refrain: Give us to-day our dai-ly bread.__ Give us to-day our dai-ly bread.__

May we be ev-er sa-tis-fied with what is our share.

Give us to-day our dai-ly bread.__ Give us to-day our dai-ly bread.

May we be nev-er sa-tis-fied 'til what is on earth is e-qual-ly shared.

Words and music © 2003 Bret Hesla

(Omit bass run, last time)

200

Flower of Compassion (#2)

Slowly, gently

Call:
1. Flow'r of Com-pas-sion,
2. Blos-som of Love, you
3. Del - i - cate Fra-grance,

All:
1. Bloom with - in, bloom with - in,
2. Draw us close, draw us close,
3. Drift be - yond, drift be - yond,

Call:
1. Flow'r of Com - pas - sion,
2. Blos - som of Love, you
3. Del - i - cate Fra - grance,

1. bloom_____ with - in each heart.
2. draw_____ us close to - ge - ther.
3. drift_____ be - yond all bor - ders.

Let All Hearts Unite

Let's Leave Our Fears and Comforts Now

Words and music © 1999 by Bret Hesla

birth. It's on - ly fair for all to share the
heart; And as the vi - sion's lift - ed up, di -
greed . That some re - ceive and some let go and

rich - es of___ the earth. The rich - es of the
vi - sion falls___ a - part. Di - vi - sion falls a -
all get what___ they need. And all get what they

earth, O peo - ple, the rich - es of the earth.___ It's
part, O peo - ple, di - vi - sion falls a - part.___ And
need, O peo - ple, and all get what they need.___ That

on - ly fair for all to share the rich - es of___ the
as the vi - sion's lift - ed up, di - vi - sion falls___ a -
some re - ceive and some let go and all get what___ they

earth.___
part.___
need.___

Listen

Other refrains:

Watch-ing, watch-ing for glo-ry yet un-seen.

Lis-ten, lis-ten. The in-vi-ta-tion comes.

Turn My Heart To Peace

(Tune: Silent Night)

1. Silent night, holy night,
All is calm, all is bright.
Now I lay me down to sleep.
I pray to God my soul to keep.
Turn my heart to peace.
Turn my heart to peace.

2. Silent night, holy night,
Wish I may, wish I might
Trust the words I claim to believe.
Learn to give as I have received.
Turn my heart to peace....

3. Silent night, holy night,
All is calm, all is bright.
Hear my prayer, God, hear my song.
As I wake with each new dawn,
Turn my heart to peace....

4. Silent night, holy night.
All is calm all is bright.
God who calls us to love our foes.
Help us heal this world of woes.
Turn my heart to peace....

5. Silent night, holy night.
God of love, all unite.
Change our fear to community.
Change our pride to equality.
Turn my heart to peace....

May We Awaken

Note: Each verse is sung twice to begin, then a third time after the corresponding bridge.

O Compassion

O God, You Will Show Us the Path of Life

Words and music ©1987 Larry Dittberner, 651-330-8930. Used by permission.
Keyboard accpt. © Bret Hesla

For each new verse, substitute the following words in place of the words "path of life":

2. City of Hope   3. Day of Grace   4. Way of Peace

211

Stream of Mercy Never Failing

Sweetly rolling

1. Stream of Mer - cy nev - er fail - ing, here we
2. Em - pty pro - mi - ses di - vide us. Em - pty
3. Keep us mind - ful of our one - ness in your
4. Stream of Mer - cy, flow up - on us. Come and

stand and look to you. Pour your pre - sence now up -
goals stand in our way. We re - nounce the ma - ny
wa - ter's wide em - brace. Give us eyes to see our
green our wilt - ed vines. We are thirst - ing for your

on us. Come and christ - en us a - new. You have
"is - ms" that turn "we" to "we and they." We ack -
kin - ship ev - ery - where in ev - ery face. May we
jus - tice. Now your realm our on - ly wine. Give us

Note: These lyrics (8787D) also work well with the tune, "What A Friend We Have In Jesus."

Words and music ©2000 Bret Hesla
Keyboard accpt. Bret Hesla and Tom Witt

named us all your peo - ple. You have birthed us as your
now - ledge our in - volve - ment. We have all di - vi - ders
learn the way of Je - sus, learn to chal - lenge and to
cour - age to be faith - ful. May we know we're not a -

own. You've re - stored us, whol - ly fam - i - ly, in your
been. Make us heal - ers of di - vi - sion, as your
serve. May we learn to live to - geth - er, lov - ing
lone. Give us joy in our re - un - ion with our

Spir - it flow - ing down.
fam - i - ly we de - fend.
all with - out re - serve.
sib - lings fin - al - ly known.

(last time only)

(D.C.)

213

We Shall Be Peace

(4 part round)

We shall be peace. We shall live in peace. Take it to the whole wide world a-round. We shall be peace.

Words and music ©1987 Larry Dittberner
Keyboard accpt. © Bret Hesla

Web of Beauty

Where There Is Hatred

1. Where there is ha-tred, Where there is ha-tred, Where there is
2. Where there is sor-row, Where there is sor-row, Where there is
3. Where there's op-pres-sion, Where there's op-pres-sion, Where there's op-

Call: (second time only) Lis-ten to my prayer, O God.

ha-tred, let me sow love. O God, let me sow
sor-row, let me sow joy. O God, let me sow
pres-sion, let me sow free-dom. O God, let me sow

Lis-ten to my prayer O God. Lis-ten to my prayer O

love. O God, let me sow love. O
joy. O God, let me sow joy. O
free-dom. O God, let me sow free-dom. O

Words: St. Francis of Assisi
Adaptation and music ©1999 Bret Hesla

Yea, O God

(3 part round)

Slowly, with reverence

Verse lyrics:

1. Yea, O God, you are our moth-er.
You are our moth - er and fa - ther.

2. We are the clay. We are the clay.
We are the clay, you are the pot-ter.

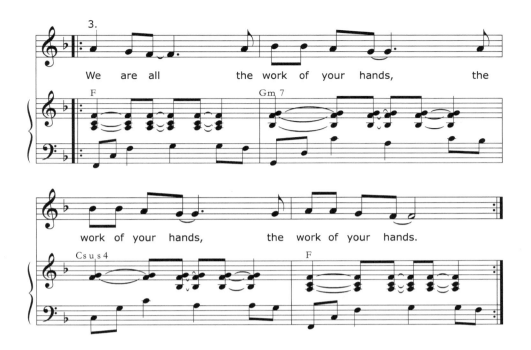

3.

We are all the work of your hands, the work of your hands, the work of your hands.

F

Gm7

Csus4

F

A Dazzling Bouquet

dazz - ling bou - quet of ev - ery kind of
all bloom to - geth - er in___ one___
ten - tion to ev - ery bud___ and___
freed from our judg - ing and___ ex -

flow - er. Jump in the vase, 'cause
gar - den: A car - ni - val of
blos - som. Let ev - ery face come
clu - ding. Just look a - round en -

we've got space for more.
fra - grance and de - light. *(Refrain)*
grace the grand bou - quet. *(Refrain)*
joy the love - ly view. *(Refrain)*

Notes:
  1. *Use a songleader to support the singers on the melody.*
  2. *This melody is loose: don't try to follow the notes too perfectly.*
  3. *Try using fiddle, guitar and accordian, with Zydeco dance beat*
  4. *Have fun.*